AWAK...
ART...

The Glastonbury Zodiac
Diameter: 11 miles

Illustration by Scott Guynup, with acknowledgement to Katherine Maltwood for her discovery of this ancient earthwork in modern times.

AWAKENING ARTHUR!

His Return In Our Time

Page Bryant

Foreword by Geoffrey Ashe

Aquarian/Thorsons
An Imprint of HarperCollinsPublishers

The Aquarian Press
An Imprint of HarperCollins*Publishers*
77–85 Fulham Palace Road,
Hammersmith, London W6 8JB

Published by The Aquarian Press 1991
1   3   5   7   9   10   8   6   4   2

Page Bryant asserts the moral right to
be identified as the author of this work

A catalogue record for this book
is available from the British Library

ISBN 1 85538 071 4

Typeset by Harper Phototypesetters Limited,
Northampton, England
Printed in Great Britain by
Mackays of Chatham, Kent

This book is dedicated to William Blake . . .

And did those feet in ancient times
Walk upon England's mountains green
And was the Holy Lamb of God
On England's pleasant pastures seen?

And did the Countenance Divine
Shine forth upon these clouded hills
And was Jerusalem builded here
Among these dark Satanic mills?

Bring me my bow of burning gold
Bring me my arrows of desire
Bring me my Spear! O clouds unfold!
Bring me my Chariot of Fire!

I will not cease from mental flight
Nor shall my sword sleep in my hand
Til we have built Jerusalem
In England's green and pleasant land.

WILLIAM BLAKE

CONTENTS

ACKNOWLEDGEMENTS

Few books come together without the help of a great many people, and this one is no exception. Throughout the past four years my studies of the Arthurian legends and various commentaries on the subject have led me to come across several books that have made a particularly strong impression on me. Of these, I am especially grateful for *The Secret Tradition in the Arthurian Legends* by Gareth Knight. Anyone wishing to obtain in-depth information regarding the Atlantean esoteric tradition and the implications of the Arthurian archetypes would benefit tremendously from Knight's book. Another valuable work that puts the Arthurian legends in an easy-to-read form and offers excellent commentary on the esoteric and psychological interpretations of the myth is *King Arthur and the Grail* by Richard Cavendish.

The extent of my knowledge of the history surrounding King Arthur I owe almost entirely to the works of Geoffrey Ashe. I am especially appreciative of Geoffrey's openness to the idea of an American writing on the Matter of Britain, and thank him for his encouragement and for his willingness to write the Foreword for *Awakening Arthur!*

Special thanks must go to my husband, Scott, and my friends Don and Mark for listening to long readings of the manuscript throughout its various stages of development. I would also like to thank Scott for his patience and support in helping to make this book a reality and for the great grilled cheese sandwiches that he fed me during the last hectic days of this project.

Heartfelt gratitude also to my literary agent and friend, Wabun Wind, for her continual encouragement and for her unconditional willingness to share her literary expertise with me for this and other projects.

FOREWORD

It is a pleasure and a privilege to comment on Page Bryant's remarkable study. Those who have been involved with Arthurian matters will know how dauntingly hard it has become to say anything new. Here, however, something new is said.

The author has made it clear what she is chiefly dealing with: not the historical basis of the legend, not the growth of Arthurian romance, but the inwardness of the main story as it is known and loved. While this means that the books she discusses principally are those of Geoffrey of Monmouth in the twelfth century and Sir Thomas Malory in the fifteenth, I am pleased to see that she values other versions, especially the one recently created by Persia Wooley in her novels of Guinevere. To my mind these are among the best of the modern treatments, and it is good to see attention drawn to them here.

What Page Bryant offers is a wise evaluation of the legend as perennial myth, with applications to our own lives today. I am especially impressed by her exploration of the shamanic background of Merlin. It makes a major contribution to a way of thinking which others, myself included, have found illuminating. She is generous in her citation of my own work. I sometimes disagree with her, but where so much is a matter of interpretation, such disagreements don't signify.

Page's reflections on the theme of Arthur's return, and how it might happen, are most stimulating and may prove prophetic.

Geoffrey Ashe

PREFACE

Throughout the research and writing of this book I encountered a personal 'initiation' that consisted of the various degrees of trauma involved in being faced with a task, of my own creation, that became much greater than could be accomplished through my limited intellectual knowledge of the Arthurian legends! So I am thankful to Geoffrey Ashe, Richard Cavendish, Gareth Knight and R.J. Stewart for their wonderful writings which were so helpful to me. In my struggle to learn as much as I could of the legends themselves and, at the same time, try to gain further understanding of the archetypal and esoteric meanings and truths concealed within them, I found it very difficult to make King Arthur and the various Arthurian characters 'mine'. Finally, I came to a point where I decided I must allow myself the freedom of embracing the characters and abandoning my strong need for validation of my own thoughts and ideas in respect of the Matter of Britain. In doing so, I found validation at every turn of my research and personal experience with these wonderful legends. The turning point came when I finally realized that 'my' King Arthur was the legendary one and not the historical figure whose existence scholars have sought to prove or disprove. Other writers – Geoffrey Ashe, for example – have written such books and have written them well, and to them we should be grateful. I wanted *this* book, however, to make a statement about the human side of Arthur; I wanted to see, and help my readers see, the path of life outlined and preserved within the legends and characters in the Matter of Britain, to show how the perils of a time gone by are still the perils we face today – and, above all, I wanted to celebrate the return of King Arthur as a 'new' beacon of light that shines in the window of the future. I will leave it to my readers to decide the merit of this work for themselves.

Fragmentation necessarily precedes unity. Fifth-century England was, without doubt, a fragmented and torn land. Leaderless and desperate, the beleaguered Britons found themselves in constant battles to ward off persistent onslaughts of Saxons. Since the departure of the Romans, they were ill-equipped and ill-prepared to defend their country. As they fought for survival and to maintain control over their land, the situation was chaotic indeed.

It was during these troubled times that two sons of King Constantine returned to England. The brothers were Aurelius Ambrosius and Uther Pendragon. Their father had been made king of Britain after coming from across the sea to save the country from invading barbaric forces. Upon his death, Britain had come under the rule of the conniving Vortigen. He, in turn, was eventually dethroned by Aurelius, the rightful heir, who sought to strengthen the British dynasty and unite the country under proper rulership. This quest was taken over by Uther, on the death of his brother, sealing the name Pendragon forever in British history.

The ever-present mists that roll over the British moors hide far more than the rugged landscape – for centuries they have swallowed any trace of the actual events and truth of those ancient transitional times of early history. What really happened was left to the somewhat questionable historians of much later times to record – and their writings seem to 'create' a history as much as they chronicle one. So it was that the imagination of romantic writers became fact, their views accepted, and even clung to with a tenacity fuelled as much by wishful thinking as by objectivity. From the fog of doubt and confusion and hodgepodge of ruthless characters there emerged a figure who was no ordinary man: Arthur, a Celtic Briton, the son of Uther Pendragon. It is his legend which comprises, in the words of William Blake, 'the acts of Albion [Ancient Britain] applied to a prince of the fifth century'. Fact or fiction, Arthur has reigned on the literary stage as an illustrious warrior-king for the past 1500 years! He remains an eternal mystery figure, mercilessly enshrouded by the passing of time. There is but one thing of which we can be certain: the tales of King Arthur and his knightly court embody an even greater mystery than the merely historical one.

The Arthurian legends have universal appeal. They are not only intriguing but also controversial. It seems as if no one can agree on any 'facts' about the king who has become larger than life – which ultimately leads to the question: did Arthur exist at all? Written sources of information that could perhaps provide proof are few and difficult to interpret, and this has left room, it seems, for writers and historians to interpret the story of Arthur to suit their own opinions and purposes. With current scientific advances that aid the field of archaeology, however, it is probable that, eventually, the question of Arthur's existence *will* be answered. Yet whether he proves to be myth or reality, the legends about his reign should not be dismissed. The story is much too valuable for that . . .

That King Arthur has been around for a long time is evidence of his popularity, a popularity that has increased rather than diminished over the years. Among the oldest Arthurian writings are those of the Welsh monk, Nennius, to whose work was added *The Annals of Wales*. As the stories were told and retold, Arthur became well established as a Welsh warrior-hero. By the end of the eleventh century there arose a collective body of legends that included *The Annals of Wales* and *The Mabinogion*, which largely consists of tales which are partly mythological and partly taken from the French romances. Because of its popularity, *The Mabinogion* had, by the early twelfth century, firmly established Arthur within and beyond the boundaries of the Celtic world.

Although there are but few definite 'facts' concerning Arthur, what there is cannot be overlooked if we are to gain a true knowledge of the king and his life. To begin with the time in which he lived: one of the two major writers on the subject, Geoffrey of Monmouth, places Arthur roughly between AD 440 and 480. What sources Geoffrey drew upon for his conclusions are unknown and his account is filled with lavish exaggerations. However, to say that he created Arthur out of nothing is doubtful. An additional point is that there was a sudden appearance of 'Arthurs' in the sixth century, all of whom were the subject of popular songs and stories. This suggests, by inference, that the literary king we know was a real person.

Another 'fact' concerns Arthur's nationality: he was not English. Described by Geoffrey Ashe as a 'proto-Welshman', Arthur was a Celtic Briton who was 'created by a gradual blending of several heroes, real or imaginary'.

Although working from this basis, in this book, as I have

already stated, I have chosen to accept the fantastic monarch as he has been popularly portrayed, rather than search for evidence for the historical king. I allow Arthur to be the king I discovered within the myths, for this allows us to explore this intriguing figure with a freedom that permits us to pass in and out of the historical, real world and the worlds of imagination and fantasy with equal ease.

Based on what we can glean from the legends, I think that the times of King Arthur were as important as the monarch himself, for it was the turmoil of those times that allowed such a figure as Arthur to emerge.

By the fifth century, England had long been a cradle of western spirituality. The well-known writer on mythological themes, Lewis Spence, states in his book *The Mysteries of Britain* that 'the island of Britain was the seat of the development of a culture and a secret tradition of extraordinary vitality and individuality'. When all the available archaeological, esoteric and mythological data is collected and organized, it will become clear that British mysticism is indeed ancient – and a great deal of that tradition continues to this day.

A major part of the mystical flavour of England came from an ingredient that must not be overlooked in our overview of Arthurian times: the Druids formed the very core of Britain's esoteric teachings and practices. Born of an ancient pagan spiritual culture, they were magicians and priests whose temple was Nature itself. Druids are said to have been the builders and/or users of many of the megalithic monuments, such as Stonehenge, sprinkled throughout the British Isles. During the late period of Roman occupation in Britain there was a strong pagan revival, and a resurgence of the Druids and their rituals was a major part of this rebirth, for they embodied beliefs and practices that had long nourished the population. Therefore, even though most of the ideas concerning the Druids should be classified as mystical nonsense, the priesthood nevertheless forms part of the backdrop to the Arthurian saga. Christianity and Paganism existed side by side for a time in Arthur's Britain, and Paganism is reflected in the legends primarily through the figure of Merlin the Magician and the Lady of the Lake, High Priestess of Avalon, whose reputations were unsurpassed in the ancient world. By the end of the twelfth century the Druid priesthood had declined, but until then there existed a strange marriage of the 'old' and 'new' religions.

So it can be seen that fifth-century Britain was a land 'in transition'. It was a grey time in history, and so long ago that the actual events and historical characters have slipped into the realms of uncertainty. What we do know for certain is that the Romans held most of Britain under their rule from about AD 40 until the fourth century, saturating the country and its people with their moral culture and with Christianity, which altered the very fabric of English civilization. When they left, the land fragmented into tiny kingdoms, each ruled by its own king. Thereafter, the Celts, who were the original people of the British Isles, sought desperately to once again assume power over their land and society. Their task was not an easy one.

The Celts, comprising tribal people from Wales, Ireland, Cornwall and Brittany, were primitive and pagan by nature. With their return to power, the long battle between their Paganism and Roman Christianity began, a battle that would have no clear winner. As mentioned earlier, the two opposing social and spiritual factions existed, for a time, side by side. Since neither could truly vanquish the other an interesting thing happened: two Christianities emerged! One was distinctly Roman Catholic, with bishops and saints and loyalty to Rome as its spiritual capital; the other might best be defined as 'Celtic Christianity', for it was strongly coloured by pagan beliefs. This form of Christianity emerged in monasteries rather than dioceses and its authority rested on the shoulders of abbots rather than bishops. Whether one considers Celtic Christianity as Christianized Paganism or paganized Christianity, there can be little doubt that the religion of these ages long past had an elusive and odd flavour.

This spiritual transition that Britain was experiencing was closely connected with her cultural and political changes, and all three proved difficult. The partial and short-lived change from Roman culture back to native Celtic life saw English civilization revert back to some of its roughest ways. Yet the knowledge, religion and skills gained during the years of Roman rule would forever influence the country – as would the ideas of the subsequent invading forces, making the post-Roman period truly a shaky time.

Transition is, though, the bedfellow of change. And rising from the confusion that change brings, new order is established. This rarely occurs, however, without the old outgoing order and the new incoming one engaging in perilous conflict. So it was in fifth-century Britain. The conflict between Celtic shamanism and Christianity tested ownership of the land as well as the spiritual, social, political and cultural values and laws. What died in the war was dead forever. What survived lived on in new and different forms, but lived nonetheless. The reversion to pagan ways and tribalism stopped somewhere in the middle between the old and the new. From the fusion of many diverse elements was born a united kingdom with a new hope for the future.

It was due to the life of King Arthur that this came to be. But perhaps from the very beginning, the king's brilliant reign was doomed to suffer a tragic fate. Before that fate was realized, however, Arthur and his fellowship of brave knights burst forth from the written page in a brilliant splendour of adventure and glory unmatched in the human drama.

The legends tell of a journey that I believe was, ultimately, a spiritual one, a journey of living and dying, of success and failure, idealism, treachery, battle, love, honour, and loyalty and betrayal. My purpose here is to consider King Arthur and his knights as possessing a special key to human destiny. The Arthurian epic goes beyond providing mere entertainment for the imaginative minds of readers over centuries of time. It is also a 'path' for living, rich in esoteric symbolism and *archetypal* mythology, embodying a hidden system of spiritual values. In the difficult and changing times in which we are currently living, it is of tremendous importance to be on a chosen and specific spiritual path of personal choice involving special dedication and commitment. Life's way is an obstacle course filled with pitfalls and hidden traps, each of which can result in setbacks, personal trauma, disillusionment and failure. But the true spiritual seeker knows that at the end of the path is the success that greater self-awareness and enlightenment brings. In order to expand our understanding further, a spiritual path becomes a way of life, fuelled by expectation, desire and need – the need to know ourselves, both individually and collectively. I feel that knowledge of the arcane symbolism and archetypal characters contained in the Arthurian legends can provide an extremely valuable tool for personal growth and awareness. A system of ethics and a full body of ancient esoteric tradition can be derived from a clear understanding of various Arthurian symbols such as Excalibur, the Round Table and the search for the Holy Grail, as well as from the adventures and challenges of the characters themselves.

We will explore here the history and meanings of these symbols and characters, discovering how they are as applicable to our lives today as they were so long ago. The Arthurian saga is a great reservoir of Celtic legend and mythology that not only embodies a great part of esoteric tradition but that also embraces the mysterious forces that govern Nature, life, and the essence of humanity. By a thorough examination of our individual selves we can discover the 'Arthur' within us – the leader, the hero, the unifier, the peacemaker, the warrior, and the conqueror, arrogant to the proud, but kind and gentle to the meek. We shall see how other major personalities in the myths – Lancelot of the Lake, Merlin, Queen Guinevere, Morgan le Fay, to name but a few – also embody powerful archetypal human qualities that reside within the human consciousness, and how these characters lead us down a path of life that we can and still do walk today. We will see how the knights' search for the elusive Holy Grail is but a reflection of our own present-day aspirations for the highest human potential.

In my attempt to retell the legends of King Arthur I was, at first, confounded by their complexity – primarily due to the many versions, their varying geographical locations and the cultural differences imposed by the authors over the years. Therefore, I have chosen to rely mostly on the work of Sir Thomas Malory, author of *Le Morte D'Arthur*, and Geoffrey of Monmouth, author of *The History of the Kings of Britain*, as well as some of the more modern versions of the myths such as Marion Zimmer Bradley's *Mists of Avalon*. I have recounted the most significant parts of the various legends, where relevant, so that the reader who is less familiar with the adventures may be provided with an adequate background, and for those who are more familiar with the Matter of Britain, I hope that reading the legends again be delightfully refreshing. I have used the most popular spellings of the characters' names and have tried to indicate, whenever feasible, the part of Europe and the British Isles from which the particular stories and characters have come.

Ultimately, I hope that my readers will be able to move these wonderful legends out of their Dark Age setting and into their rightful place within the human mind and heart so that they might serve as teachers to us as we make our own journey from birth to death. The jousts, combats, dragons, fairies and various knightly ventures are but metaphors for the struggles and battles of our own lives. The values of courage, loyalty, and honour displayed in the Arthurian tradition have not been cheapened by circumstances nor tarnished by the passing of time. They stir our hopes for immortality and make us long to score a defiant victory against death, the last enemy. And, above all, in our present age of uncertainty, I believe that the Arthurian themes have a particular urgency and appeal for our understanding. Through *Awakening Arthur!* we can join together in the search for integrity and make an attempt to discover and realize our true and best self. With Arthur's help we can put meaning into our lives. We can appraise our ideals. We can find purpose in the conflicts we must bring into balance. Life's journey is not unlike any other journey, no matter the time or distance involved. It begins with the first step. So, let us take that first step – let us begin.

1

ARTHUR
The Man and the Myth

If King Arthur did not live, he should have.
SIR WINSTON CHURCHILL

Myths are clues to the spiritual potentialities of the human life.
JOSEPH CAMPBELL

The weather-beaten stone towers of Tintagel Castle reached up into the night sky as if they could touch the very stars that foretold the future of Britain. On that fateful night the starry figures of the Crown, the Dragon, the Archer, the Hunter and his dogs, the Great Bear and the Pleiades hung brightly in the indigo heavens over the rugged Cornish coast on the south-western British peninsula. Inside the castle walls the first cries of a newborn infant could be heard. They were the cries of one who would come to be called Arthur,

Artorios, the Boar, whose birth had been foretold – and who, 15 years later, would ascend the throne of Britain and preside over a time of adventure and glory as an ideal leader, renowned warrior, and defender of the Celtic kingdom. Perhaps there are those born whose fate is sealed from the very beginning, the coming life's circumstances arranged by the soul prior to birth, those who are aided and protected by spirit forces whose task it is to watch over a life that is to be one of service to humanity for ages to come. Such a soul, so it would seem, was King Arthur.

There are many roads into the heart of the Matter of Britain. One is the avenue of history, whose demand for the 'facts' of its personalities and events and chronological sequences seems almost cruel in the face of time so long past. There is also the road of legends, that frees 'historical' figures to live on the lips of bards and on the pages of faded manuscripts . . .and, finally, there is the road of myths, myths that spin a web of fantasy and delight in the minds and hearts of young and old as one generation gives way to another in an unbroken line of those who are nourished by the manna of adventure, splendour and intrigue.

The life of King Arthur satisfies all these. It possesses the 'facts', though they be at times elusive, of which history's documents take notice. It also has all the colourful threads needed to weave a wonderful legendary tapestry. And, whether fact or fantasy, the myth of a king, set within a medieval setting, and the events and people that surround his life has been around to entertain and inspire for 1500 years!

Arthur, the actual man, has been pursued for centuries by historians. But, as already stated, whether he existed or not is really of no ultimate concern here. Rather, it is the Arthur of *myth*, born from the shadows of a deep and veiled past, who is the subject of our attention. It is *his* story that has held the interest of untold minds. This is the Arthur who was spirited away by the wizard Merlin to be raised incognito in a neutral household until his true identity could be known; it was he who, when all others failed, pulled the sword from the stone, and by doing so, unknowingly revealed himself to be the rightful heir to the throne of Britain. It was this Arthur who reigned over the kingdom from Camelot and who founded the illustrious Fellowship of the Round Table, 'the bravest fellowship of chivalrous knights ever to dominate a battlefield and support a throne'.[1] And it was this Arthur whose reign was to suffer a tragic fate when his beautiful queen and his bravest knight fell in love, plunging the king and the kingdom into division and despair. This is the Arthur who legend tells us lies 'sleeping' somewhere in Britain, awaiting a time when, once more, his country has need of him – for it is then that he will come again to win the battles that must be won and conquer the foes who must be conquered because they threaten the sanctity of Britain's peace and well-being.

King Arthur's life unfolded amidst a time when Britain was divided into many lesser kingdoms, each ruled by a chieftain who both defended and presided over his domain with the fierceness of a bold warrior. These were perilous times when the beleaguered country was struggling to recover its own identity from years of Roman occupation and to protect itself from ruthless invaders who would claim the land as their own. One of these minor kings was Gorlois, Duke of Cornwall, whose castle at Tintagel stood as a grey slate bulwark on the time-carved cliffs of the Cornish coast. Tintagel was home to the Duke, his court, the lovely Duchess, Igraine, and her daughters, one of whom was Morgan, who would herself come to rival Arthur in fame and memory. During this time, Uther Pendragon held the

British throne. His advisor was Merlin, whose magical skills set him as far apart from ordinary man as Arthur would be from ordinary king.

In a meeting with Gorlois at Tintagel, Uther Pendragon first encountered the lovely Igraine. His feelings for her were the proverbial 'love at first sight', which soon turned into an uncontrollable obsession. Determined to have a romantic rendezvous with the duchess, Uther enlisted help from Merlin, pleading with the wizard to work his magic for him so that his overwhelming desires might be satisfied. Merlin agreed, with the condition that, for reasons unknown to anyone but himself, any child born from the unholy union would be turned over to him at birth. Uther accepted what must have seemed an unusual condition, as he would have, no doubt, accepted any condition that seem even half reasonable, given his state of mind.

Merlin's magic wove its web of illusion that not only satisfied Uther's passion, but, ultimately, changed the course of British history. The magician's objective received a stroke of luck when, conveniently, Gorlois was called away to battle. His absence provided the perfect opportunity for the enraptured Uther, aided by Merlin's magical skill of shape shifting, to assume Duke Gorlois' physical appearance so he could easily gain entrance into Igraine's bed chamber.

With their coupling, Arthur was conceived. Then, when word came of Gorlois' death in the battle that was going on at the very time when Igraine was with Uther, the duchess realized what had happened! She was filled with an anger that surely must have been mixed with grief and guilt. Nonetheless, Igraine was later to wed Uther, fulfilling his dreams.

The tales that grew up around the sexual union of Igraine and Uther Pendragon have been told and retold. Granted, they began with the story of the magically contrived sexual liaison. But, on more subtle levels, that union is indicative of a much more subtle one: the union between spirit and matter, Christianity and Paganism – and the 'powers' that are generated by the interaction of and that are present within both.

Shortly after birth, Arthur was, as promised, given over to Merlin, who turned the newborn child over to one we know only as Sir Ector. Ector's real son, Kay, and Arthur were raised as brothers, and neither of them knew Arthur's true identity or parentage. Aside from his well-rounded and contented life as a member of Sir Ector's household, the young Arthur was also tutored by Merlin in the ways of the Old Tradition and the magical arts, instilling in Arthur's overall character an intriguing dimension and, firmly establishing both his pagan and Christian 'connections'. In a few short years, Arthur had learned well and had matured into a strong, healthy youth. Merlin then knew that it was time for the future king to find out who he really was, so that he might begin to fulfil his human destiny. So the magician set the wheels into motion by arranging events that would lead to that revelation. In the meantime, Uther Pendragon had died, and since his death, England had been without an effective leader and without a true and rightful heir to the throne. No one man had been able to unite the country or its people under one banner of loyalty. But this was about to change.

Around Christmas-time, Merlin called the nobility of the country together in Londinium (London) upon the premise that the identity of the real heir and next high king would be forthcoming. While the assembled nobles were attending Mass, a four feet square marble stone appeared in the churchyard. In its midst, the huge stone contained an anvil of steel which had a sword stuck in its middle. The sword was engraved with the words: 'Whose Pulleth out this Sword of this Stone and Anvil is Rightwise King Born of All England.'[2]

Though many tried, none succeeded in freeing the sword. Then young Arthur was asked by his brother Kay to go and fetch him his sword, and went to his sibling's quarters but could not find the blade he was looking for. Fearing he would seem incompetent, while the others were away, he went to the churchyard, strode up to the sword in the stone and pulled it out with ease! He gave it to Kay who recognized it immediately for what it was and, knowing the impact it would have, tried to claim that it was he who had removed the sword and should be proclaimed the rightful heir and king. But Sir Ector, thankfully, realized what was going on and quickly put a stop to Kay's deception. The sword was put back into the anvil so that all who wished to try to rescue it were given another chance to do so in front of witnesses. Once again, only Arthur succeeded. His true royalty was revealed.

During this time, Celtic Paganism, which had long been deeply ingrained in the consciousness of the people, was experiencing a 'rebirth', while Christianity, the new incoming religion, was gaining prominence as the dominant faith. In light of this, there is an interesting side note as to the symbology that many writers claim lies concealed within the presence of the sword in the stone in this important event in Arthur's life. The sword is given to represent justice; the stone, Christ. If we assume that this is valid and add to it the fated youth's Christian birthright and the throne's allegiance to the new religion, this incident would firmly establish Arthur as the Chief Defender of the Faith who would rule Britain by unquestionable *divine* right. On the other hand, his association with Merlin, his magical conception, and his learning of and proving his true identity by the same means, and his tutelage in the Old Religion made Arthur a true heir-apparent who could be a king for all the people, pagan and Christian alike. Perhaps only such a man could have succeeded in coming to the throne and have any real hope of rallying *all* the people around him in support.

When Arthur began his reign, he faced what would turn out to be several years of fighting jealous foes who challenged his claim to the throne. But with the help and advice of Merlin, his magical sword, Excalibur, and its enchanted scabbard to protect him, and his own skills as a warrior and strategist, Arthur won out over all his enemies, earning both respect and glory. Through carefully planned battles he regained control over more and more territory and expanded his domain; then, after a time, peace began to settle over the land. This first objective achieved, Arthur was then faced with a new kind of war: his own high-spirited warriors began fighting with each other for personal prestige and reputation and to win a special closeness to their king. To solve this conflict, Arthur turned his full attention towards establishing the Order of the Knights of the Round Table, ushering in the splendid Age of Chivalry and giving rise to some of the most illustrious knights the world has ever known. Because of its implications and effects upon society, it is important that we take a look at chivalry, which formed the backdrop to all courtly affairs.

Romantic writers of the Arthurian saga did not allow real events or historical dates to get in the way of their story-telling, as pointed out by Geoffrey Ashe: 'Whatever the actual period of the story, they updated it, dressing it up in the costume of their own time, introducing castles and heraldry and tournaments and chivalry and literary love-conventions'[3] and the advent of chivalry was no exception. Actually indicative of military status, chivalry embodied certain rules and principles that formed a 'code' of living, a code of ethics, battle, and human behaviour. Granted, it was only the knights who took the vows of chivalry, but the entire court was subsequently affected by it. Chivalry clearly defined what was expected of a knight: he must, first and foremost, love God with a love strong enough for him to be willing to lay down his life if need be; he must possess a strong sense of loyalty and justice and have a love and desire for peace; he must keep the mind, body and heart pure and not indulge in lust and/or trivial activity. Honesty and frankness were valued highly and treason and false judgement were never tolerated. The chivalrous knight should swear to protect the poor and the weak alike. He must respect and be the defender of all women. Gluttony was a sin. So was pride. And attendance at daily Mass was expected not just of the knights, but of everyone, for the court was, on the surface at least, Christian through and through.

One of the most powerful results of chivalry was what became known as 'courtly love'. This idea of love put a woman on a pedestal, so to speak, and she was served by a man or men whose pleasure and satisfaction were derived from that service. But there was a problem – 'true' love was not required for this, nor was it guaranteed to evolve from chivalrous behaviour and attitudes. If true love were indulged in, then its physical and emotional demands could, and most likely would, be far stronger than those of chivalry itself. We shall see evidence of this in the ill-fated romance between Sir Lancelot and Queen Guinevere. Under the code of chivalry, the court, the king, and society as a whole must come before individual desires and needs. While this may seem a great personal sacrifice, the honour a knight would earn in return for faithfully following the code would make it all worthwhile.

Undoubtedly, it was the *ideal* of chivalry that made the

system work. Certainly there were those who abused it by embarking upon adventures for the sole purpose of personal glory and/or for the indulgence of individual desires. Such behaviour, sooner or later, would in fact destroy the system, for it defeated the purpose of the ideal. But it certainly added colour to the already colourful lives of the characters in the Arthurian epic.

Returning to Arthur's life, there is the tale of his sexual encounter with Morgause, wife of the Scottish chieftain, Lot. Unaware that she was his half-sister, Arthur made love to her, and his son, Mordred, was conceived. The reader should also note that certain modern versions of the legends have made Morgan, not Morgause, the mother of Mordred, his conception taking place at Avalon during Beltane before Arthur is aware that Morgan is his half-sister.

However, when the high king was told by Merlin that Mordred would destroy him, the Fellowship, and many of his knights, Arthur was deeply troubled. He tried to prevent the prophecy from coming true by sending for all the children who, according to Merlin, had been born on May Day, the day of Mordred's birth. The ship carrying the babies born in Scotland was wrecked during its travels. But, unbeknown to anyone, Mordred survived, to appear, years later, and fulfil the dreaded prophecy.

Let me pause here once more from the story of King Arthur's life, though, to consider an important lesson that we might learn from what we have seen of his character thus far that specifically involves his methods of handling *authority* and *power* over other people. Though few of us will have the actual experience of being in the position of a king or queen, all of us will, in our own ways and through our individual experiences, have to learn how to deal properly with *authority*. Perhaps some of us will find ourselves in positions of authority in our professional lives, while others will be in similar circumstances within the family unit as parents or even as elder siblings. We might also, upon occasion, experience having authority within friendships and through associations with others. Regardless of the specific situation, how we handle our position of authority will no doubt determine the outcome of these relationships. And when possessing authority over others, our *motives* will ultimately determine how we will use the power inherent within it. Selfishness and personal gain are perhaps two of the most frequent reasons why people misuse that inherent power. If we are to have true ethics we must go beyond our individual desires and motivations to take 'the whole' into account, whether 'the whole' be a company or business, a family, a community, a nation (as in the case of King Arthur), or even the entire planet. Yes, unlike Arthur, today we have to think in *planetary* terms – and ours is an endangered world. Knowing how to deal properly with *personal power*, on all levels of our lives, no matter what form it takes, can help us tackle what we must and give us a deeper understanding of why we are the way we are, both positively and negatively. Only then can we change what needs changing. Except perhaps during conflicts with his enemies on the battlefield, Arthur always showed tremendous concern for how others felt and related to him. You will remember that it was precisely his concern for equality among, and in fairness to, his knights that he founded the Fellowship of the Round Table. He was first a friend and secondly a king. No one was singled out, no one was given special favour.

Upon the founding of the Fellowship, Arthur's life became an adventure filled with knightly challenges against demons, dragons, fairy enchantresses and purely human foes. Together with Merlin, his advisor and friend, he conquered enemies and preserved the sanctity of the kingdom. It also was during this time that two other individuals came into the king's life who were to change it forever: Guinevere and Lancelot du Lac. Arthur needed a wife and the kingdom needed an heir. Upon meeting the lovely Guinevere, Arthur chose her at once to be his bride. A maiden of Roman-British descent, Guinevere was reared in Cornwall, the daughter of Leodegran (Leodegrance) of Carmeliade. She and Arthur were married at Camelot in a ceremony filled with all the splendour of royalty. Some say that the queen's dowry included the Round Table that was to become the centre of Arthur's court. Afterwards, the ideal couple began what should have been an ideal union and life but which was, sadly, doomed to become one of pain and betrayal.

Some versions of the legends say that Lancelot, a man from western France, was sent to escort Guinevere and her entourage to her wedding with Arthur, while others say he came shortly afterwards. In any case, the handsome youth was first brought to the court by the Lady of the Lake, who had reared him from infancy after he had been orphaned by the death of his father, King Ban of Benoic. Lancelot then became the greatest of all Arthur's knights. No man could match his physical prowess as a jouster and fighter, and none was more handsome than he. Adored by the women and admired for his knightly skills by the men, it was Lancelot who became Arthur's defender and most loyal supporter, his true 'brother'. His respect and love for the king were legendary – as was his love for Arthur's wife, Guinevere. It is hard to know just exactly what drew these hapless lovers together but it was their relationship that sealed the fate of the Fellowship and doomed the kingdom. It was their love that hurt Arthur and pitted him against Lancelot, ending a friendship whose roots were planted in the soil of admiration and loyalty.

When Arthur finally realized that he could no longer deny the adulterous relationship between his best friend and his wife, he swore revenge on Lancelot and vowed not to stop until 'the flower of chivalry of all the world was destroyed and slain'.[4] A battle ensued that split the Round Table into those loyal to Arthur and those loyal to Lancelot, a battle that, in truth, neither of them wanted. But, even though Lancelot tried to convince Arthur that he had never dishonoured the queen, the king refused to listen. During the battle, Lancelot had the opportunity to kill Arthur but he did not. Realizing the futility of his feelings, he told Guinevere that she must return to Arthur. The sad lovers parted and Arthur told Lancelot never to set foot on British soil again. Yet even though the knight and his followers went to France, Arthur followed him to continue the fight, putting Mordred, his illegitimate son, in charge of Guinevere and the kingdom.

Mordred fell in love with Guinevere and set out to figure a way to have her, and the kingdom, for himself. He hatched a plan that he was sure would work by forging a letter that would appear to have been sent from Arthur to Guinevere. In this letter, 'Arthur' told of having been mortally wounded by Lancelot, and said that the war was over and lost, that Mordred should become king and that Guinevere should be his wife. Knowing the true nature of Mordred, Guinevere ran away and took refuge in the Tower of London. From there she sent a messenger to France to find out the truth of Arthur's plight. If he were indeed dead, she wanted Lancelot to come and rescue her from Mordred, who continued to besiege her.

In France, the war had come to a stalemate. Seeking peace, Lancelot offered to go into exile for a decade. In this way he hoped to spare his own life and the life of Arthur and Gawain, who had become the king's closest knight and supporter after Lancelot had accidentally killed his brother, Gareth, in battle. The past could then be forever put behind them and forgotten. Though Arthur seriously considered accepting Lancelot's offer, Gawain would not. The battle continued to rage, and during it Lancelot had the chance to kill Gawain, but, once again, he refused and walked away. Gawain later died in a battle in which he and Arthur were helping to defend Burgundy against a Roman invasion.

Finally, Guinevere's letter reached Arthur and the king swore to strike down his treacherous son. Upon hearing of Arthur's plans of returning, Mordred gathered his own army to fight against his father. Guinevere took an opportunity to escape the Tower and went into the safety of a nunnery on Salisbury Plain.

Upon landing at Dover, Arthur was met by Mordred and his forces. Influenced by a dream the night before in which Gawain had appeared and told him that if he fought against Mordred he would be killed, Arthur tried to make peace with his evil son. A truce was drawn up and Arthur and Mordred, each accompanied by 14 knights, met to sign the treaty, which gave Mordred the territories of Cornwall and Kent and also guaranteed him succession to the throne upon his father's death. Neither side trusted the other and when they came together, nerves were tense. It all fell apart when one of the knights drew his sword to kill a serpent that had slithered out from beneath a nearby bush. The ensuing battle was the most ferocious that Britain had ever seen. It went on all day and many lost their lives. When all but a few on both sides were dead, an enraged Arthur took a spear and ran it through his deceitful son. Knowing he was doomed, Mordred gathered his last strength, raised his sword and brought it down on Arthur's head, piercing his brain.

The knight Bedivere took the body of the wounded king and laid it under a tree by a lake. Arthur instructed Bedivere to cast Excalibur into the water and, reluctantly, the knight agreed. A hand came out of the lake, grasped the sword and took it into the dark water. As the dying king lay upon the ground, there came out of the mists a barge carrying robed and hooded queens who took Arthur to the Holy Isle of Avalon. Some say he would die there of his mortal wounds, others that he would be healed. In any case, we never hear of his final breath. Into the mists Arthur disappears, into the mysterious realms of our imagination and memory. So ends the physical saga of Arthur the King, his life drawing to a close as mysteriously as it began.

And so begins the unravelling of the true meanings, both symbolic and archetypal, of this legendary king of the Dark Ages. Arthur's life is filled with experiences we all must encounter and lessons we all have to learn. He embodies archetypes that can, when defined, serve to guide and direct us into a better understanding of ourselves, as individuals, who must meet and overcome the challenges, both positive and negative, that life brings, and through which we may learn and grow.

First, however, it is important to consider the term 'archetype' and its implications regarding human nature. The Swiss psychoanalyst, Carl Gustav Jung, left us with a wonderfully enlightening legacy that evolved from his work over a period of some 60 years. One of the most profoundly revealing aspects of that work concerns Jung's hypothesis of a 'collective unconscious' which is perhaps best described as a non-personal part of the human mind. Often misunderstood, the collective unconscious is not evidence of some sort of 'group soul'. It is, rather, a theory that accepts that all human minds have a common foundation. One of the unique features of this collective unconscious is that it is a *hereditary* part of human consciousness and an integral part of the 'whole self' that is composed of a reservoir of latent images or pictures that Jung called 'archetypes'.

Archetypes are inherited from our ancestral past and include both human and animal traits. Jung taught that even though archetypes are separate image structures in and of themselves, they can and do form combinations which he called 'clusters'. These clusters, in turn, are responsible for what he called 'complexes' which greatly affect our individual behaviour, in a positive or negative way, depending upon our individual response to them and the nature of the complex to begin with. Once we come to understand the existence of the collective unconscious within ourselves, we can then come to understand the two basic functions archetypes perform when, through our personal experiences in life, they are triggered into effect.

The first of these functions is based on the idea that archetypes are universal in nature and that they have existed since the remotest of times. This implies that everyone inherits the *same fundamental archetypal images*, which provide an interesting link between all human beings. Various archetypes are awakened at critically significant times during life. Through the influence they have on our personal views and perspectives, as well as upon our behaviour, we can gradually become aware of new and different possibilities for ourselves and new reasons for living. Viewed this way, archetypes are truly a hidden source of energy and power. However, a lack of awareness or basic understanding of their existence and presence within our consciousness can lead to our being driven by their influence, totally unaware of their effect on us or their contribution to who and what we are.

The second function of archetypes involves the supposition that these primordial images give us our *individual predispositions and potentialities* for experiencing and responding to the world around us. Individual fears, likes and dislikes, talents, phobias, and aversions or attractions to certain things and or kinds of people are examples of this important function.

Some examples of archetypes – keeping in mind that they number in the thousands – include the hero, the warrior, the martyr, the child, the trickster, the magician/shaman, God, Mother Earth, Father Time, the knight in shining armour (which may have come from the Lancelot character being thought of by the masses as the proverbial 'knight in shining armour'), Satan, the wise old man or woman, the crone, the god and goddess, and the 'Bogey Man', to name but a few. Keep in mind that each embodies a concept and model for the term used and from which others are copied. For example, any man who is the ideal male is a woman's 'knight in shining armour', and a beautiful and intriguing woman is often called a 'goddess'. Sometimes, in our modern society at least, 'products' can also become archetypal for all items of a like type, such as Kleenex becoming the archetype for all tissues. Also, there are archetypes that are elements and powers in the natural world such as magic, wind, fire, water, birth and death. Special objects can also be archetypal, as we will see later with the Holy Grail and Arthur's magical sword Excalibur. It must also be borne in mind that it is the *combinations* of archetypes, the 'clusters', that give Jung's theory life. Take as an example a person who has the 'God', 'power', and 'trickster' archetypes functioning deep inside him or herself. The result of this cluster would be a person who would be prone to use religion and God as tools of expressing personal egoic power and who would likely seek to gain personally from the prestige, attention, self-righteousness, money and control over others that might be gained from the activities this archetypal cluster can instigate. It is highly possible that no one would be the wiser as to what was really motivating such behaviour, including the person involved, unless he or she were *conscious* of the specific archetypal patterns operating inside. In short, whatever archetypes are active within our own individual lives, they set up patterns of behaviour born from a common inheritance within our minds and consciousness.

Turning to the character of King Arthur, there are two archetypes that may be easily detected: the warrior and the hero. Both of these affected Arthur's behaviour and dictated his motives. They were triggered into life when he became king. Though different, the warrior and the hero have certain similarities, and both provided the power that drove the greatest of the men in the Arthurian saga: King Arthur and Sir Lancelot. Becoming aware of these energies and their effect upon the lives of these two men can go far in helping us to discover them and their effects within ourselves. At this point, I shall consider the archetypes in relation to Arthur.

A warrior is one who fights in battle. But we have to go beyond this simple definition in order to discover the deeper qualities that are inherent in the warrior archetype. Arthur not only fought for a 'cause' but he also embodied the cause: the kingdom. And he did not fight alone – he did not have to, for he was able to unite his men together into an undefeatable force which was dedicated to the throne, to himself as king, and to his vision of an England united and at peace. Achieving this was no small task even for a monarch. To have vision is one thing, but to have that vision be contagious is another. Yet Arthur achieved his goals. History is filled with men and women who have possessed this special kind of charisma, whether they used it for good or evil purposes, and this, combined with the force and skills of the warrior, made Arthur a human force to be reckoned with.

Arthur was also a hero who was admired for his bravery and for his noble deeds. Whereas the warrior focuses on power, usually over others, the hero focuses on his superb ability to *affect* the masses. He defends the people and himself and, more importantly, he changes the world into one of his *own* image. Arthur did both. Camelot became *his* world, a world of his *own* making; and Camelot, in and of itself, has become an archetype that represents the ultimately romantic domain of courtly splendour, within which can unfold legendary characters and tempestuous relationships. Many will recall that the White House under the presidency of John Fitzgerald Kennedy was called 'the American Camelot'. We are each the creators of our own world. We must each fight our own battles and defend our own causes and give birth to our personal 'vision'. Finding the hero and the warrior within ourselves is one of the ways to ensuring the fulfilment of these needs. Further discussion of the warrior and hero archetypes will be offered in a later chapter that concerns Lancelot.

Due to the unusual circumstances surrounding Arthur's birth and death, and because both 'birth' and 'death' are archetypes, I feel they also deserve a mention here. Perhaps it is easier to understand what is meant by the 'universality' inherent within all archetypes by considering birth and death, for all that lives has been born and will die. Together, these two archetypes embody the great 'cycle' of rebirth which affects all life forms on Earth. In fact, cycles form the very essence of the laws of Nature.

Although born of mortal parents, the circumstances of Arthur's conception and birth were anything but ordinary, having been made possible by Merlin's magical intervention. When we view this event from a purely physical perspective we, of course, realize that this is the stuff that legends are made of and nothing more. However, if we view it from a *symbolic* one, we can see much more. Merlin's involvement added a mystical, 'otherworldly' dimension, not only to the intrigue of the legends but to Arthur's character, elevating his position and increasing his personal magnetism in the minds of readers throughout history. He was a 'fated' child, one meant to be. Further intrigue comes when we look at other events that happened prior to Arthur's birth. You will recall that the future king's birth was foreseen. In *The History of the Kings of Britain*, Geoffrey of Monmouth states that shortly after the death of Aurelius Ambrosius, when Uther Pendragon came to power, there appeared a portent in the sky in the form of a star and a dragon, with rays of light shining forth from its mouth. One of the rays shone out over the land of Gaul (France). Merlin interpreted the omen as a sign of Aurelius' death. He further stated that the ray indicated that Uther would have a son who would some day lead the Britons across the channel as conqueror and king. In fact, it was because of that portent that Uther came to be known as 'Pendragon', which translates to mean 'head dragon' or 'dragon's head', indicating a military leader. In this way we have Merlin playing a real role in the destiny of the kingdom and those at its helm. He knew from that moment on of Arthur's coming and, with his magical assistance in his conception, the magician helped to bring about the event he himself had prophesied.

From this legend, two things come to mind. The first concerns the similarity of the prophecy to that of another child that was to come to the world stage over 2,000 years ago. Now, don't misunderstand me. It is not my intention to compare the person of King Arthur with that of Jesus in the literal sense. However, there are some interesting parallels between their physical appearances on the Earth that may make a statement about the entrance of all individuals who are destined to change mankind and/or history in some positive way. Both births were foreseen and, within the prophecies, the role and purpose of the predicted one was clearly indicated. Jesus the Christ was a messiah who came to save mankind. Arthur was also a 'messiah' who came to save a besieged nation and its people. Each task was monumental, with its own special conditions, and each would surely require a person with special potentials and qualities.

Also, both conceptions occurred under interesting conditions. Jesus was, according to scripture, conceived by a virgin, whereas Arthur was conceived by an 'arrangement' of magical proportions. Both fly in the face of biological law. One of them came to save the country, the other a world. Another link between these two lives concerns the fact that Arthur's true identity was concealed from him until it was time for him to assume the throne of England at the age of 15. The Bible leads us to understand that the identity and purpose of the boy Jesus was also not recognized by himself or others until around the age of 12.

Certainly the magical circumstances of both of these conceptions and births were symbolic of the workings of a Higher Force or, at the very least, of the appearance of an important individual. Perhaps when the world reaches a critical point in evolution, a 'saviour' is sent to show the way and, in doing so, he or she helps to assure the unfoldment of a Divine Plan. On a less than planetary scale, at the time of Arthur, Britain had come to such a critical point. The country needed a 'saviour' in order to survive and he came in the form of King Arthur. Symbolically, the similarities in the conception and birth of Jesus and Arthur serves to link further the medieval king with the Christ, which may have elevated him in the eyes of the Christian court and won him allegiance from those who might otherwise have opposed his accession.

When we turn our attention to the death of King Arthur

we find equally curious circumstances. To begin with, as noted earlier, there is no definite statement concerning Arthur's death. Rather, he is taken to Avalon where, some legends say, he was healed of his wounds – a sort of resurrection perhaps. There are also stories that have him 'sleeping' until the time when he will return to save Britain. These incidences are reminiscent of similar circumstances and predictions surrounding the life of Jesus as the Christ. All of these similarities become highly suggestive of there being some sort of Christian mysticism contained within the Arthurian Matter of Britain along with, as we shall see later, the legends being the embodiment of an ancient Mystery School and the teachings inherent with the same.

Also, there is the matter of Arthur's grave site, or, more appropriately, the lack of it! In the versions of the legends that have Arthur actually dying, it is said that he met his death at the time of the Winter Solstice, in the dark, cold season of the year. But where the fallen monarch was laid to rest after his death has remained a mystery, for no grave marker has been proven to be authentic. However, I must digress at this point to discuss information that may have some bearing on the mystery of Arthur's grave. It seems that there are those that not only believe that the king died but who also claim to have found the location of his burial.

In AD 1191 a Welsh or Breton bard was said to have told King Henry II of the site where Arthur, along with his queen, Guinevere, was laid to rest: at Glastonbury Abbey in Somerset, beneath a slab of stone in a large hollowed-out oak log. Allegedly, on the underside of the stone was found a lead cross inscribed with Latin words which, when translated, read: 'Here lies buried in the island of Avalonia, the renowned King Arthur.' Both the cross and the bones discovered by the abbey monks of the time have since disappeared. The bones are reported to have been placed in caskets and, in 1278, put in a black marble tomb before the high altar of the abbey, where they remained until the abbey's destruction during the reign of Henry VIII. Today, only a small sign marks the spot.

Personally, I dismiss this alleged grave site as a fraud. In King Henry VIII's day, and in the times leading up to it, churches, abbeys and monasteries were big business. The faithful made pilgrimages to such sites to pray and celebrate the faith. Places that possessed highly revered relics such as the bones of saints or other great people drew pilgrims en masse. With them came money and other riches, which were given freely in acts of personal contrition and in support and for the maintenance of these sacred sites. Needless to say, much of the wealth found its way into the pockets of the abbots and monks until Henry put a stop to it by destroying, for his own purposes, many of the monasteries and abbeys, and claiming their wealth for the throne. Glastonbury Abbey was the wealthiest of them all and its power would have been greatly enhanced by the 'discovery' of Arthur's grave. For this reason, and since no real evidence has survived, the finding of Arthur's grave all seems too contrived for me to judge the Somerset grave site as anything other than a hoax.

In *The Landscape of King Arthur*, Geoffrey Ashe writes:

Most historians, though not all, have dismissed this affair as a fraud and a publicity stunt. It happened soon after the fire, when money was needed for rebuilding. King Arthur's grave would attract visitors and donations, so King Arthur's grave was duly concocted. Another motive was perhaps to discourage the Welsh in their resistance to the kings of England, since if Arthur was demonstrably dead, he would not be coming back to aid them.

In all fairness, however, there is no evidence that the

Glastonbury monks used the supposed grave site for either of these purposes. Furthermore, there are several scholars, including Ashe, who are not so quick to dismiss the grave site as a fraud, leaving the mystery and ultimate truth of its authenticity for time to unravel.

The lack of a physical grave, or conclusive proof of its whereabouts, however, is not the only problem involved in trying to untangle the circumstances surrounding Arthur's death. Most of the legends tell of the king being spirited away, you will recall, to Avalon to be healed of his wounds. The likelihood of literal truth in this legend is faint. But it does – and this is our true concern – contain subtle innuendoes that have become an integral part of the mystique of this episode of the Arthurian romance. Arthur is taken away by the Lady of the Lake who, at the time, was his half-sister, Morgan le Fay. As will become clear later, Morgan's character, for the most part, is that of an evil sorceress who is jealous of Arthur and wishes to do him harm. In the end, however, she is his healer and possible 'saviour', perhaps signifying that the king has finally come into balance with the feminine forces in Nature and perhaps also within his own inner self, a concept that I shall pursue later in much greater detail. The reader will also recall that after the battle where Arthur received his mortal wound from Mordred, Bedivere was reluctant to toss Excalibur into the water. Although this too is an event that embodies a great deal of symbolism, I shall, for now, simply note its importance as marking the ending of the kingship.

Arthur himself is but one of many characters and adventures that come to life on the pages of Arthurian manuscripts. The seeker can discover within the Matter of Britain a full bubbling cauldron of ancient knowledge that is as applicable today as it was then. 'This is not a superstition that has no value to our own age. It is to our mortal peril that we abandon a subconscious wisdom acquired over thousands of generations, of whose true sources we can have but an intuitive feeling.'[5] When we approach the archetypal images that are concealed within these medieval myths, they will, for each individual or group 'polarize and amplify any inherent weakness or corruption within themselves'.

As we see Arthur being taken to the Isle of Avalon we know that he disappears within us into the mists of the unconscious, the inner Otherworld. This final scene conceals several important *initiatory* experiences that, again, all humans must undergo. Arthur's mortal wounds were not really from the sword of Mordred but from the evil that exists within us all, including Arthur himself. It is that evil that brought down the Round Table. It is that evil that results in the Great Mysteries being hidden from us, that makes God and Goddess at odds with each other, and that separates Heaven and Earth. Mordred is the greed, jealousy, egotism, negative anger and lust upon which feeds our fear of loss and lack. The battle between the king and his treacherous son is the battle that rages between our own base self, or ego, and our soul. And, just as Arthur destroyed Mordred with his own hands, so must we, as individuals, take our weaknesses and faults into our own control and accept responsibility for conquering them for ourselves.

With King Arthur clearly in our minds, let us go forward from this beginning and explore that cauldron of ancient knowledge that is indeed still there for us to use today, as the Arthurian archetype reawakens to save us from our 'mortal peril'.

References

1. *King Arthur and the Grail*: Richard Cavendish.
2. *The Landscape of King Arthur*: Geoffrey Ashe.

3. *Mythology of the British Isles*: Geoffrey Ashe.
4. *The Landscape of King Arthur*, op. cit.
5. *A Primer of Jungian Psychology*: Calvin S. Hall and Vernon J. Nordby.

MERLIN

Lord of the Forest, Counsellor to Kings

Merlin is the figure glimpsed at the heart of the Matter of Britain, and how dearly would one love to sit where he sat, gazing at the wild creatures of the woodland, and looking upwards at the starry mysteries he sought to penetrate.

NIKOLAI TOLSTOY

Merlin exploded onto the literary stage 1500 years ago as a master magician who has since come to personify all practitioners of the magical arts. Wizard, prophet, stargazer, high priest and advisor to kings, he 'typifies wisdom from a source that is not personal or human, yet applied to humanity both individually and at large'.[1] A pagan living in a predominantly Christian society, Merlin was recognized as a great seer and Lord of the Forest who guided the order and purpose of kings, foretold the future, and preserved the sanctity of the magical arts. To some he will forever remain nothing more than a purely literary character born from the fantasy of mere mortals. But to others he is the primordial shaman who helped to make the cosmos accessible to humans – in human terms. Through his skilful use of the magical arts, Merlin warded over Britain. Through the pages of the Arthurian legends he blazed a trail of magic, wonder and power as the one who may very well have been the last heir to the pagan priesthood. In the words of author John Matthews, 'Nowhere is the *inner nature* [italics mine] of the Arthurian Tradition more clearly focused than in the figure of Merlin.'[2]

In the earliest legends of Merlin's life, the wizard is portrayed as the personification of the Lord of the Forest. Dressed in the antlers and skins of the wild creatures of the woodlands, the magician was adept at dealing with the raw primordial forces of Nature and had a special magical kindredship with the wild boar, the wolf and the stag. In the Arthurian tales Merlin takes on the image of the robed enchanter whose arcane knowledge and skills afforded him the performance of many prodigious feats. Both of these images are due mostly to myth-makers, but each contains some degree of legitimacy, though neither are entirely correct. There was never a Merlin such as the one who leaps forth from the legends of King Arthur, just as there was no real Arthur who fit the literary descriptions attributed to him.

The legends of the great wizard were actually based upon a real-life Welsh bard and seer named Myrddin who lived in the sixth century in northern England. The Myrddin of these legends and texts is much different from the popular picture of Merlin. He first appears in the writings of Geoffrey of Monmouth in his *Historia Regum Britanniae* (The History of the Kings of Britain) of 1135. In the *Vita Merlini*,

Geoffrey's second Arthurian book, Myrddin, reduced to misery and madness, is found living in the Caledonian Forest, a formerly wooded area located in southern Scotland. Tradition links Myrddin with the infamous battle of Arfderydd which was fought in what is now Cumbria. During this battle, the king of the British dynasty of Strathclyde, Rhydderch Hael, defeated and killed the Cumbrian chieftain, Gwenddolau, who was Myrddin's lord. The horror of the battle and a feeling of personal responsibility for the deaths of his leader and so many others drove Myrddin to insanity. He fled into the dense and blessed sanctity of the woods where he lived for years as a wild man. Some say that it was his madness that actually helped him acquire the art of 'seeing' into the future. Myrddin's life in the forest was described as something less than pleasant: he was alone, his daily life spent as an outcast who knew hunger and suffered the severity of the elements. How he must have longed for bygone days when he was surrounded by those he loved and when he was needed and admired by his lord and countrymen alike!

Geoffrey of Monmouth transformed Myrddin into the popular Merlin, and in doing so he gave us the most celebrated character of the Arthurian epic, with the possible exception of King Arthur himself. From the moment of his appearance, this Merlin possessed great magical powers unmatched by any magician who had come before, and he became counsellor and seer to four British kings.

The first of these was Vortigen. It seems that this unruly king had problems with the Saxons whom he had brought to Britain as mercenaries. After fleeing to Wales, Vortigen was advised by his court magicians to build a great tower that would serve as a safe haven for him and his subjects. The chosen site, allegedly in Snowdonia, proved to be the source of enormous frustration, for each time its foundation was laid, it sank into the ground! The court magi consulted their oracles and informed Vortigen that the only answer to the problem was to find a boy who had no mortal father. If the unfortunate lad were sacrificed and his blood sprinkled on the foundation of the tower, it would stand. Relying on this advice, the beleaguered king sent out men to find such a youth.

Vortigen's search was rewarded when the young Merlin was found living in Carmarthen. He was reputed to be the grandson of the King of Dyfed, but had no mortal father. When brought to Vortigen's court, the outspoken youth immediately attacked the competency of the magi by informing their king of a pool of water which lay beneath the foundation of the tower and was causing it to sink. He also told of two hollow stones that were at the bottom of the pool and said that inside them there were two dragons, one white, the other red. Upon digging, the pool was found, as were the two stones. When opened they revealed the dragons, who immediately engaged in a battle which Merlin interpreted as being prophetic of future trouble between Britain, the red dragon, and the Saxons, the white dragon. This battle would rage until the coming of one who would be called 'The Boar of Cornwall', who would defeat the Saxons heartily and assume the high throne of Britain. This 'Boar', of course, would be Arthur. This was to be the first of a string of prophecies attributed to Merlin by Geoffrey of Monmouth, and it set the stage for the appearance of the one who would change the course of British history.

The next two kings who would benefit from Merlin's advice and magical guidance were the two brothers, Aurelius Ambrosius and Uther Pendragon. By this time, Britain had come under the jurisdiction of the Christianized Roman Empire. Merlin, matured into a seasoned shaman, had by this time been credited with marvellous achievements, one of which bears mention here for it gave rise to a rumour that has persisted to this day, linking him with Stonehenge. The story runs that Merlin commanded that the stones of Stonehenge be dismantled and taken from their original place in Ireland and rebuilt on Salisbury Plain in southern England to serve as a monument to Britain's nobles slain in a massacre by the Saxons. Although these events are highly unlikely, the tale did serve the purpose of establishing Merlin's link with Stonehenge and thus with pagan traditions. Long associated with magical rites and secret traditions, Stonehenge was, and still is, the most celebrated pre-Christian monument in Britain. Through this association, Merlin, who in modern texts has been portrayed as a Christian mystic, [3] is seen to have a foot in both religions domains. This allows the seer to move in and out of both worlds as a valuable asset to Christian kings and pagan priests and priestesses alike.

After the death of Ambrosius, Uther Pendragon came to the throne. Surely no feat performed by Merlin surpasses his transformation of Uther, by magical means, into the likeness of the Duke of Cornwall, Gorlois, so that he might couple with the duchess, Igraine. Ordinarily, such a use of his power would fall squarely into the category of black magic. But when we consider Merlin's prophecy that foretold of the appearance of Arthur, we can see the reasoning behind the magician's willingness to arrange Uther's rendezvous with Igraine. He knew what the outcome would be; he knew his magic would serve far more than the momentary satisfaction of human lust – that it would, ultimately, shape the evolution of British history.

So the fourth monarch Merlin served was Arthur himself. Although Geoffrey of Monmouth says little about this phase of Merlin's life, other writers have take full advantage of the gap by painting a picture of him as Arthur's advisor and magical helper. Geoffrey Ashe writes: 'The result was a great literary Creation, and a remarkable one. It was as if Merlin had indeed been latently a god all along, blossoming out in romance as divine once again, the sponsor of Britain's Golden Age.'[4]

Some of the events credited to the magician during this time include arranging for Arthur to receive the enchanted sword, Excalibur, from the Lady of the Lake, and designing the Round Table, which came to symbolize the spiritual heart of the Order of the Knights. It was also Merlin who, allegedly, laid the groundwork for the beginning of the quest for the Holy Grail.

With his knowledge of the stars, herbs, incantations and divination, along with his ability to create magical illusions, Merlin would be, no doubt, an asset to any king, and throughout the legends he never loses his intrigue. We are repeatedly informed of his magical skills and the role he played in the life of Arthur's court. But there is much about him we do not know. For example; where does he live? He seems to appear out of the blue only to vanish again to a place somewhere – but nowhere. His home was not Camelot, this much we do know, but he has no castle, no identified domain save the forest which, as we have seen, is linked more closely with the earlier character, Myrddin, than Merlin. Similarly, no age is ever given to the magician. No time or method of death is ever described. The reader is left to assume he died in the tower where he was imprisoned by the enchantress from Avalon, Nimuë. Whether deliberate or not, these omissions only add to the mystique of this intriguing character. We know enough but never too much so that the wizard must forever remain outside and beyond the reach of any definition of the 'ordinary' or any usual psychological interpretation. For us, Merlin must remain shrouded in the mists of time and our imagination.

When we pursue the legendary Merlin figure from an *archetypal* perspective we gain a valuable insight which we, as individuals, may use to come closer to understanding one of the most profound 'energies' that, if and when it awakens within us, can lead us to unravel the deepest meanings of life. We are reminded in the words of Nikolai Tolstoy that archetypes 'are embedded in man's unconscious mind since first he developed the power of rational thought'. Merlin, as archetype, 'epitomized man as part man and part beast and, at the same time, a Saviour who conveyed the spark of Divinity'.[5]

All myths, in one way or another, reveal the state of the human condition at any given time. Through the figure of Merlin, we come to know of the existence of the powers of the cosmos and to the recognition that we, as individuals, can access these powers for the purpose of manifesting what we need and desire, and to align ourselves with the whole of Nature. R.J. Stewart points out to us that 'Merlin held the seeds and wisdom for the forthcoming age which we can have seeded in our imagination if we ask for it in the proper manner.'[6] But we must open our minds. To truly apprehend and understand the egoic qualities of Merlin and come to understand his powers, we must abandon the narrow approach of pure rationalism which keeps the 'cosmic' out of reach. We have to turn away from thinking that the scientific method is the only source of real knowledge. If and when we do this, we can then rely on Merlin to reawaken our unconscious so that we might reach deeper inside ourselves.

The current times are right for this inner searching to occur. At various times throughout human history, mankind has been on the brink of disaster in one form or another. During such times nothing goes right: disease is rampant, crime surges and war seems to be constantly imminent. Just when everything appears to be out of control and decline seems irreversible, something happens either to *give* humanity the necessary tools of insight or to pressure people into *acquiring* them for themselves. When employed, these tools of awareness can then help society to re-establish itself on a more positive and constructive course. We are currently experiencing, globally, such times of uncertainty and fear. The world faces an ecological, social, economical, political, and even spiritual crisis. Perhaps it is the existence of technology, our space-age magical wand, that makes this particular crisis in human history more threatening than most – technology being responsible, on the one hand, for the devastating weapons we have at our disposal and for much of the dangerous toxic wastes of our industrial society; while, on the other hand, for the advances of modern medicine and the wonderful methods of communication and travel that have made the world a much smaller place. In many ways, technology has indeed played a role in the very formation of the values of our modern society and times. But we have become dependent on technology – it *is* our magical wand, possessing the power of both 'saviour' and 'destroyer'!

In the past, times of crisis brought forth the appearance of an incarnate Master who held the key to the wisdom of the ages, a sort of avatar who set humankind on the 'quest' for the self-knowledge necessary to change values and solve the problems. Merlin was such a figure. He knew the ancient teachings. And, unlike many such figures, he was one in whom pagan tradition and Christian mysticism were blended. Merlin preserves the ancient spiritual tradition which is, as suggested by Gareth Knight, 'after the old Atlantean model'.[7] Upon this, the modern aspirant can draw so as to gain greater self-awareness.

There may very well be evidence that this return to the

Old Ways is happening at this time and that mankind has come to an evolutionary turning point. Since the early 1960s there has been an explosion of interest in various aspects of occult wisdom. Astrology has attracted millions of followers, while numerology, the Tarot, esoteric psychology, various forms of meditation, and personal psychic and spiritual development have formed the foundation for alternative lifestyles for individuals and groups alike, worldwide. Over the past 30 years, the search for more and related knowledge and the desire for greater awareness has given rise to countless articles and books on subjects that range from Jungian psychology, with its special emphasis on dream interpretation and the contents of the human psyche, to those which are concerned with the existence and work of the angelic kingdom and the world of spirits.

While these different subjects have each captured the spotlight at a given time, we are currently experiencing a surge of interest in shamanism. The reasons for this apparently vary from person to person; collectively, however, the reason for this interest lies in the fact that the ways of the shaman offer the aspirant knowledge and ceremonials that can help him or her live a fuller, more balanced life in the face of the perils of the current times.

A definition of the shaman and his skills given by the widely acclaimed anthropologist, Joan Halifax in the book *Shamanic Voices*. This may also give us some clues as to why shamanism is experiencing such widespread popularity and acceptance:

> *The shaman, a mystical, priestly, and political figure emerging during the Upper Paleolithic period and perhaps going back to Neanderthal times, can be described not only as a specialist in the human soul but also as a generalist whose sacred and social functions can cover an extraordinarily wide range of activities.*

Shamans are healers, seers, and visionaries who have mastered death. They are in communication with the world of gods and spirits. Their bodies can be left behind while they fly in unearthly realms. They are poets and singers. They dance and create works of art. They are not only spiritual leaders but also judges and politicians, the repositories of the knowledge of the culture's history, both sacred and secular. They are familiar with cosmic as well as physical geography; the ways of plants, animals, and the elements are known to them. They are psychologists, entertainers, and food finders. Above all, however, shamans are technicians of the sacred and masters of ecstasy.

We can see by this definition that the shaman had it all in terms of position and authority within his tribal community. Various forms of this arcane knowledge have been handed down from generation to generation so that the ancient knowledge of a given lineage or tribe has been preserved and the wisdom itself kept alive. It is this wisdom that is being sought out by huge numbers of people now.

The methods by which this view of reality is achieved involve various spiritual practices designed to 'open' the mind so that entry can be gained into other, more subtle, realms of reality. In a world where the bogus is often passed off as real, people are looking for truth in both the knowledge itself and in those who practise it. As a result, practitioners from various cultures are being sought out by those who wish to become apprenticed to *credible* Eastern gurus, Wiccan high priests and priestesses, medicine men and women, and others who are involved in secret orders and societies that are based upon ancient shamanistic traditions. The time appears to be right for the shaman to reappear at centre stage, for he has something to give the masses to help us come to a deeper awareness of the world around and within us. Armed with such an awareness, we cannot help but begin to change our values to make a real and positive difference in the present condition of the planet and human society.

It is thus little wonder why people from all over the world are responding to the urgency of the need for change and are experiencing the awakening of the Merlin archetype within their own inner nature. It is the shaman's view of Nature and his skills that can help bring about a reconnection between man and Nature. It is indeed the right time for this; and perhaps the urge to know of the forces in Nature, of spirits, and the ways of seership is even going a step beyond the sole need for knowledge which we can apply to these times of peril. In a world where organized religion has often fallen short of fulfilling personal and collective human spiritual needs, people have started to search for deeper knowledge of and meaningful *participation* in sacred rites rather than continuing to be content while the clergy carry them out. We want to learn of the Mysteries and take charge of applying them to our everyday lives rather than simply listening to ministerial commentaries and accepting them, whether we understand and relate to what is being taught or not.

Carl Jung, through his studies and observations of the human psyche, came to the conclusion that each of us has a built-in, subliminal need to acknowledge the supernatural powers and realms of existence. Belief in various forms of these powers has been with us since the dawn of human history and the value inherent within such a belief was also noted by Jung when he commented that those who embrace any form of transcendental philosophy and awareness are often far more capable of dealing successfully with life's stresses, pains and disappointments.

So the search is on. Everywhere there are those seeking a doctrine or philosophy that will complement and accommodate their own personal concept of those invisible 'energies' to whom they feel they can turn and upon whom they can rely in a time of crisis for fulfilment of spiritual needs. There are many individuals who, after many years of following a particular religion, have begun to recover from spiritual abuse! Religion has both elevated and corrupted the human spirit, as the pages of history show only too clearly.

Even though the knowledge of the shaman may not, in and of itself, provide the answers for all human ills, can it be left completely out of our spiritual pursuits if we are to gain a real understanding of the world around us and learn ways by which we may travel own inner landscape with greater ease? Our tribal ancestors made use of the instinctive side of human nature. Instinct and intuition were their only mental allies and their minds were untainted by the over-emphasis on logic we are expected to follow today. We seem to be regaining this instinctive awareness, and realizing more and more what the shaman has always known: there is a life force around us and within us. Shamans not only recognized the presence of this force but also knew of our dependency upon it. Therefore, a shaman would devise ways by which he could learn to communicate with it, satisfy it and honour it. He personified it. He needed to find ways to have it do his bidding whenever feasible to do so. So, ceremonials were born, sacred rites that were designed to summon 'the force' in Nature, to unite spirit and matter, and to heal and nourish the human soul. Above all, personal knowledge of and participation with the natural forces can give *purpose* to life or, at the very least, a direction by which one can *discover* and, eventually, fulfil our purpose on the Earth Mother. We must be able to 'see', not just look. In fact, the power of vision is perhaps the most profound of all shamanistic skills and is that most desired by apprentices and seekers alike. Merlin had visionary skills. He could 'see' the future. But to truly understand the many aspects true *vision* we must realize it means more than simply knowing the future.

Due to the increased interest in shamanism, particularly in Europe and the United States, teachers have begun to appear on the scene within what is generally referred to as the New Age or Alternative Thinking movements. While these teachers and their teachings come from various cultures throughout the world, none has received more notice or attracted more interest than the Native American.

American Indians refer to their shamans as 'medicine' people. 'Medicine' is a term used to label the practitioners themselves as well as to describe their particular knowledge and/or skills. These can include specific knowledge of the spirit world and certain spirits, words of power, the proper use of sacred objects and/or the meanings inherent within and the right to lead ceremonials. A medicine person may be male or female, depending upon the tradition of the tribe involved. Some tribes have secret medicine societies which focus attention on various ceremonies designed to contact and win the favour of certain spirits or to celebrate specific holy days and times when the 'power' of Nature is at its strongest. This power is called upon to ensure the prosperity of the people. For example, many Native Americans rites are conducted for the purpose of bringing rain, successful hunting, or fertility among the tribal women. Others are performed for the purpose of honouring the spirits of totem animals, who are believed to possess great powers which the shaman seeks to gain for himself. In addition, there are ceremonies to attract and honour plants and animals that provide food. Sometimes the entire tribe participates in these ceremonies, sometimes the rites are performed in secret by members of medicine societies. For the most part, these ceremonials have to do with communication with certain spirits who favour the spiritual life of the tribe.

Among the many hundreds of tribes of Native people in North America, there are some who stand out as possessing some of the most powerful medicine people and ceremonies. These include the Hopi of north-eastern Arizona and other pueblo people of the American South-west, and the Sioux and some other major tribes of the Great Plains. It is to these that modern aspirants are turning for knowledge. Many are walking the 'medicine path' in their search for personal spiritual fulfilment, a path that is sometimes called the 'Good Red Road'. In his book *Breath of the Invisible*, John Freesoul writes:

> *Sometimes folks want to learn about our philosophy or culture or religion. But there is no philosophy or dogma or doctrine with us. We don't separate religion and culture. Our way of life is life itself, a living relationship and a living realization. We call it 'the Red Road.' Living in harmony with the spirits of Nature, ceremonies, the vision quest, the sacred pipe, the wisdom of the Medicine Wheel, healing, sacred dances and chants and even some forms of art is all a part of the way of the Red Road.*

It is important to know that such widespread interest in Native American spirituality by non-Native people is something new. The American Indian has, for over a century, been down-trodden in so many ways – socially, culturally, physically and economically. Most tribes (and their spiritual traditions) have teetered on the brink of complete extinction, and almost all have been condemned to lead a miserable life. In some cases, much has been lost due to there being no one to pass down the knowledge to. Many Indians have set their ancient ceremonials aside and have followed, some willingly and some not, Christianity or other religions. The spoils of modern life have replaced the importance of the ancestral spirits and powers. But a revival is occurring! Because the Merlin archetype is awakening, the ancient traditions of the American Indians are being sought after with a zest that has not been known for many generations. With this interest has come a revival of much more than the ancestral traditions – the Native peoples' human spirit has also reawakened, and value has been restored to the teachings. Many have urged a return to the 'old ways' – a return, incidentally, that was prophesied long ago by medicine people and elders within various tribes. Although this is a valuable recovery, however slow in coming, for the American Indian, there is something else that may prove of even greater value: by seeking the knowledge and ways of the shaman, we are creating the opportunity to discover the 'power' for ourselves and we are learning how to deal with the 'magician' archetype within our personal unconscious.

Native American medicine people and their secret societies are but 'offshoots', however, of a far more ancient occult tradition that has its origins in a dim ancestral past which some say was Atlantean. With the reawakening of the Merlin archetype comes a revival of sacred orders who possess the key to the ancient wisdom.

No discussion of Merlin would be complete without an investigation of the Druids, the 'medicine' society with which he is often associated in the minds of readers, even though this is most likely erroneous.

The religious/spiritual priesthood of the Celts of the pre-Roman era in Gaul (France) and Britain was Druidism. Like most of the orders that have embodied the ancient wisdoms in their doctrines and sacred rites, the Druids disappeared from the historical scene with the advent of Christianity, only to reappear during the Renaissance in the works of classical scholars and romance authors, who, more often than not, found them convenient vehicles for their own philosophical concepts. The Druids were an élite body whose functions were wide-ranging. They were magicians, prophets, poets, judges, and even doctors in the sense that they knew of the medicinal use of plants and other methods of healing the physical body. We can see how reminiscent this definition of a Druid is to that of the shaman provided earlier from Joan Halifax's writings.

These priests often served in the role of advisors to rulers and held enough influence over them so as actually to control them or, at least, affect their decisions on political, social, religious and even inter-tribal affairs. They could therefore prevent or instigate bloody wars. Geoffrey Ashe states in his *Mythology of the British Isles*: 'Their order was not a separate priesthood but a kind of caste. Druids had wives and children. Women as well as men could belong, though not with equal status. The dominant male element was recruited from society's highest ranks.'

Druids officiated at and participated in various kinds of rituals. The oak, the mistletoe and the apple were among the plants that were held sacred, as were the stag, the boar and the wolf of the animal kingdom. The special quality of apples came from their association with fairies and the Otherworld, which were similar in importance to the Druids as the 'Nature spirits' and kachinas (Cloud People) are to the Hopi Indians, in that they were inhabitants of the realm of spirits and closely related to the forces of Nature. Apples were also believed to confer the gift of immortality and were sometimes used for divining the future.

Druid priests met in woods or among sacred groves, perhaps, at times, those of the enchanted apple trees. Like the American Indians, Druids respected certain animals because of a special power believed to be inherent within that animal. This included certain birds, such as the eagle, hawk and owl, and some reptiles, especially serpents. It is interesting to note that the serpent has been a symbol of wisdom since the earliest times, with the noted exception of the Christian serpent, who, as an agent of evil, was responsible for tempting Eve and thus bringing about the advent of 'original sin'. This was an obvious attempt, and a successful one I must say, to distort a positive and ancient pagan symbol to suit the purposes of Christianity.

The research of Geoffrey Ashe reveals that Druid apprenticeship lasted for some 20 years. Much of this time was spent in caves and secluded forests where neophytes were taught, through oral transmission, the 'charms, riddles, incantations, [and] mythical narratives'. We know that the priesthood held a vast array of gods in high esteem and that many of their rituals were for the purpose of communion with them. Although it has been written that the Druids were practitioners of human sacrifice, this is not known for certain and has been the subject of much debate. It may have been little more than Roman propaganda against the order, for with the establishment of the Roman Empire in Britain, there was 'open season' on the Druids, resulting, sadly, in their demise.

Another similarity between the esoteric knowledge and practices of the American Indian and the Druid priesthoods concerns a knowledge of and relationship with the heavens. Both groups were astronomers and astrologers, with a calendar of their own making which conformed to certain holy days and seasons. 'Druids harmonized the solar and lunar years by means of a nineteen-year cycle.'[8] Although the Indian tribes with whom I am familiar follow a normal one-year cycle calendar, their *ceremonial* year may differ: the Hopis' ceremonial year, for example, begins at the time of the Winter Solstice and ends in the latter half of July. Celestial events such as eclipses, comets and planetary movement, and certain stars were of importance to the Druids as they were, and are, to various shamanic cultures.

These points bring me to agree with Geoffrey Ashe when he points out: 'The Druid's ancestor was perhaps the medicine-man, dancing and drumming in ritual gear, conversing with spirits, wielding influence through oracular utterances and a rapport with the powers of nature.'[9] That each was heir to an ancient knowledge is evident, as is the revival of interest in what they both believed and practised.

Thus far we have been dealing with what results from the reawakening of the Merlin shaman/magician archetype in society as a whole and have determined that there is renewed interest in and acceptance of such ideas. Books like this one which deal with the subject of the ancient wisdoms appear in abundance, as do teachers and practitioners of the sacred arts. But what happens on the subtle unconscious levels of individual human consciousness if and when the Merlin archetype is triggered into life?

One of the first things that occurs is that an energy is aroused that is profound in its effect. It creates an urge to learn ancient knowledge and to seek to apply that knowledge to one's everyday life. Then, as we begin to acquire information, we also begin to encounter conditions and experiences designed and created by the inner self or soul to teach us the lessons necessary for us to be capable of using the knowledge and skills properly.

Perhaps one of the first of those lessons involves *responsibility*. Responsibility suggests a moral obligation to carry out the duties that are a part of our coming to be aware of and eventually to understand our true nature. It demands personal liability for our actions. It means that we need to give ourselves credit for our successes and that we must accept blame for our mistakes and failures – which requires being capable of rational conduct. Being responsible indicates trustworthiness and the acceptance of duties and positions of power without being blinded by power itself. Becoming a magician does not mean we can work magic for ourselves and, in doing so, make everything perfect. Quite the contrary. We, as magicians, come to know that we, as individuals, are the creators of our own reality. We must make the best of our world by taking control over our lives through recognition of, and acceptance of, our personal power to do so. The use of our power is always crucial to our growth. When, and if, we use it destructively, it becomes a tool for dominating others, and demonstrating our self-appointed superiority. Used positively, personal power becomes a constructive force in our lives that gives us a drive for success that is harmonious with others, a zest for life, and self-control. Thus, responsibility comes with knowledge and knowledge is power. We are each accountable for what we know and for the constructive use of that knowledge. Anything less is not acceptable.

Another lesson we learn from the magician archetype involves the issue of *self-trust*. How often we turn to others for personal validation. Am I making a mistake? Am I right in what I think or feel? Should I do this or that? While it is not wrong to share our ideas and feelings with other people, we cannot allow ourselves to depend upon acceptance or approval before we do or feel something that will influence who and what we are. Such dependency indicates a fear of relying upon ourselves, and sets others up to take advantage of us or to take the blame should the guidance given prove to be incorrect or harmful. We must embrace life and its obstacles. We must let down our guard and trust our own thoughts and feelings and our personal vision of reality. How can we ever truly trust someone else until we have learned to trust ourselves?

The magician learns to 'see' through the illusions of the material world. The Merlin archetype urges the development of this kind of sight so that we do not continue to waste time and energy by trying to force life into our own mould. Training ourselves to 'see' demands that we confront falsehoods in many forms. This may also result in not following the crowd, and in standing up for principles that may diminish our popularity and acceptance by others or, under some conditions, by society as a whole. Intuition may present us with information or ideas that are not in keeping with the norm, and we may be tested as to our willingness to trust in what we know and to take action based upon that knowledge.

The magician knows that force does not work and must be replaced by *discipline*. Discipline requires perseverance, courage and the skills necessary to reach a goal. The magician knows that he must flow with the tide of evolution, not against it. He must be in touch with the powers in the universe and come into balance with them so as to create a harmonious relationship with his self and the whole of Nature. Staying in touch with one's inner self to such a degree is not easy; it requires us to recognize our role and importance in the universe but not to succumb to that importance on a personality level. When armed with these important personal tools, the magician is ready for the highest knowledge, that of *magic* itself.

Magic is the art of controlling events or effects by supernatural power. But, like Excalibur, magical knowledge is a double-edged sword! Used in ignorance or negatively, it becomes a weapon of destruction. Used positively, it becomes a tool of wisdom and insight that keeps one from the harm of ignorance and imbalance. Which it will be is determined by our personal motivation and by the relationship we, as individuals, have established with the universe. When we are out of balance because we are irresponsible, or do not trust or rely upon ourselves, when we are out of step with the rhythm of the forces around us, we will likely view magic as some kind of 'quick fix'. This is when a little knowledge is dangerous, for we can become little more than dabblers in the occult arts and bring immense harm upon ourselves and others. Working with magic is not for the mere purpose of making sure that everything turns out the way we want it to. Rather, it is an awareness of powers that are greater than we are, yet still a part of us. To deal with it successfully demands that we are, first and foremost, in harmony with our own inner nature, so that we may flow *with* the universe in its evolutionary unfoldment. Understanding the truth of this statement intellectually is one thing, however – reaching and *maintaining* this level of awareness is another! The only way to achieve this is to get in tune with our inner landscape. All the world's great teachers have stressed the importance of this truth and have taught the submission of personal will to the Will of the Absolute. Only the truest of magicians realize that this does not involve giving up one's own identity or power, but acquiring an even greater sense of identity and aligning our power with that of the Higher Force.

The magician does not wrestle with his faults to try and force transformation. In *The Hero Within*, Carol S. Pearson writes: 'Instead of struggling against powerlessness, loneliness, fear, or pain, the magician accepts them as part of the fabric of life and hence opens up to discovering the lessons they bring us.'[10] This leads to conscious self-control. An old Roman saying goes 'the fates lead him who will; him who won't they drag'! We have to be willing to free ourselves from the stagnation that comes from wallowing in our human pains and not hold tenaciously onto our problems and shortcomings as if they are all we have. 'A bad life is better than nothing' or 'I am only human' are attitudes that ensure stagnation, and we must transcend them before we can hope to deal properly with or understand the magician archetype, should it awaken within.

A great portion of the magician's life and energy is devoted to the working of spells and enchantments to 'cause' things to happen. In addition, like Merlin, he relies on rituals and ceremonies, sacred objects and tools, costumes and other paraphernalia to assist him in the manifestation of whatever may be the objective of his magical practice. On the surface it would seem as if the magician himself *causes* the results. But this is a misconception. Magicians do not make things happen: they *allow* it! They create a climate within which what *needs to be* occurs. This requires of the magician not only a tremendous degree of faith in himself, but also the ability to get out of his own way!

This makes a strong case for being in absolute individual control – which demands personal discipline. Often we are so busy making proclamations about who and what we are, what we can do, what we will cause and what we will prevent, and how important we are, that the only thing we really accomplish is the defeat of our purposes. How constantly we stumble over our own words and actions! The magician, however, *lets* life happen. He attracts that which he needs, both materially and circumstantially. He trusts that he will have what is needed and does not allow himself to spend his energy in useless and depleting worry, in adopting attitudes of lack. He does not fear loss. He trusts the universe and his relationship with it so that he is open to being provided with what is necessary for a fruitful life. His confidence tells him that all will be forthcoming. His very life is an affirmation of his faith and a statement about his relationship with the natural forces. The magician knows the *laws* of the universe and that he cannot break these laws without paying the price of becoming a victim of them. Thus, the magician takes no action that disturbs the natural order of things. He takes no more than what he needs. He is aware of both his human and animal attributes and can recognize one from the other as well as the connection between the two.

The magician archetype may, however, only colour our approach to and response to such obstacles that comprise yet another test of our use of knowledge and power. Even Merlin, in spite of his magical skills, was also a human being, at least in part. He, like us, had to confront human emotions and desires.

When we take a look at Merlin, the man, we learn of his infatuation with Nimuë, one of the 'damsels of the lake'. Malory presents an unflattering image of the aging magician by portraying him as falling in lust with the lovely fairy damsel, who only uses him to learn his secrets then turns around and uses what she learned to imprison him! Other legends tell of Merlin's passion for Morgan le Fay, who, in many modern versions, learns much of her magical knowledge from him. The magician's ill-fated feelings for these enchantresses give us a look at his human self. Richard Cavendish in *King Arthur and the Grail* comments on this human side when he comes to the conclusion that 'perhaps this [infatuation] is because he was only half human and his human half was female; perhaps it is because his male nature was demonic, which made him capable of lust but not love'.

Malory not only points out Merlin's 'demonic' nature, which may be in keeping with his Christian viewpoint, but also supports the view that Merlin's plight shows the problems that a man will encounter when he gives his feelings over to a woman – a purely patriarchal perspective!

Cavendish goes on to remind the reader that 'because Merlin could foresee the future, he knew perfectly well what was going to happen, but he could not help himself'. He had indeed 'caught himself in a net of irresistible passion' that was to bring about his personal downfall. I have known good psychics and teachers who allowed their knowledge and skills to go to their head, resulting in their attracting attention and gaining power for themselves alone. All ethics are abandoned when the material world and its spoils are allowed to blind us from our hard-won understanding of reality and truth. Does Merlin, in his purely human behaviour, simply typify the type of individual who enters the spiritual path fuelled solely by a thirst for knowledge, and who is willing to spend every waking moment reading and studying at the expense of all else? Such people never seems to lack for enthusiasm and they enter the path with a zest and wilful determination that gives the *appearance* that nothing could deter them from their goals. But the energy of such eagerness often gets spent very quickly or, worse, brings a one-sided development that always ends in sad disillusionment.

To avoid this, mind and heart must work together. To take another example, just think of the trouble that Lancelot could have saved himself if he had but practised that truth, which he surely knew. The same goes for Merlin – and for ourselves, as individuals. We must work for well-rounded development and not give our power over to anyone for any reason. Time and time again I have listened to Sun Bear, a Chippewa medicine man, talk about how we give away our power. We give it to food, sex, friends, drugs, religion, a guru, or even to the idea of power itself. Merlin made this mistake in his inability to control his passion for Nimuë and it imprisoned him in a tower to which he thought only she had the key. Not so. Only Merlin himself had the key, for the tower was of his own making. From his unfortunate predicament we can learn an important lesson, which we can integrate into our personal character and lives: *we* are the creators of our circumstances, positive or negative as they may be. We cannot look to others to blame or to save us from what we have created. We can get advice. We can receive support. But, in the end, we must free ourselves from our self-built towers so that we might transcend those aspects of our human nature that threaten our growth.

Beyond the human or shamanic qualities that Merlin possessed, it was his position as advisor to the king that reveals the highest role he served as a character within the Arthurian epic. It was he who ensured the survival of the Ancient Tradition. These teachings were, and are, an immense body of occult knowledge that had been 'given' to mankind in the earliest stages of evolution on Earth and which many have described as Atlantean in origin. However, I think it would be more true to think that the Atlanteans were the last in the old civilization to have it as the foundation of their spirituality, for the true origins of the so-called Atlantean Mysteries is not known.

Atlantis was doomed both geologically and culturally, and the Initiate-Priests knew it. Before all was lost, they chose from among themselves those who would travel to various parts of the world to plant the 'seeds' of the wisdoms. That this was accomplished is evidenced by the religious, philosophic and scientific knowledge that was, and is, possessed by the priesthoods of antiquity throughout the world. These include the ceremonialism of the ancient Mayans and others in Central America, the Chaldeans, the ancient Egyptians, and the American Indians. Manly Palmer

Hall, in his monumental work, *The Secret Teachings of All Ages* states:

> *In the midst of the Atlantean program of world colonization and conversion, the cataclysms which sank Atlantis began . . . Carrying with them the sacred and secret doctrine, these Atlanteans established themselves in Egypt, where they became its first 'divine' rulers. Nearly all the great cosmologic myths forming the foundation of the various sacred books of the world are based upon the Atlantean Mystery rituals.*

It can easily follow that Merlin was indeed the one whose task it was to implant the 'seed' in the new and coming civilization in Britain, from where it would eventually spread throughout the whole of Europe. In Gareth Knight's *Secret Tradition of the Arthurian Legends* we find further confirmation of this having been Merlin's true role:

> *At the end of the Atlantean epoch Merlin was charged to bring to the new root race a more subtle and complex form of the plan. The new pattern was that of the Round Table. This has been preserved in human consciousness over the centuries, latterly through the vehicle of the Arthurian legends.*

According to Dion Fortune, Merlin brought the Atlantean legacy to Britain through the bloodline of Igraine, mother of Arthur, in whose veins therefore flowed the seeds of the 'old' and 'new' bloodlines. This duality is cleverly concealed in the legends by Arthur having both Christian and pagan connections.

His tasks completed, Merlin's departure from the legends has many versions. There any no special note of his death or his final fate, although there is mention of a tomb which is referred to as *Perron de Merlin* or 'Stone of Merlin' which, many years later, was the place from which some say Arthur's knights set out to begin their Grail adventures.

Another tale has Merlin speaking of his own deliberate 'withdrawal' so that people will believe what they see happen in the future and not think that he had brought it about. The state of the 'withdrawn magician' allows him freedom from the physical body but does not prevent him having continuing influence over worldly affairs at large. In this guise, as described by psychologist Carl Jung, he remains as 'the age-old son of the mother'. It is in this role that Merlin ascends into the archetypal realm, where he operates within human consciousness, enabling us as individuals and as collective humanity to walk the magician's path to bring ourselves towards integration with our higher nature. It is there, forever sealed in the guise of a literary character within the Arthurian legends, that he continues to play a part in the preservation of the most ancient of the wisdoms and as master of the magical arts.

Merlin's times were not unlike those in which we now live. They were days of continuous upheaval, when the threat of destruction and death abounded while the powers of rebirth and renewal struggled to assure life's very survival. Such troubled times do strange things to people and elicit peculiar reactions. In the words of the Merlin scholar, Nikolai Tolstoy: 'Amidst all this evidence of the ephemeral nature of terrestrial life, it is not surprising that people turned their thoughts to eternal truths, beside which the turmoil of war was but as the "battles of kites and crows" – as Milton derisively termed the wars of early Britain.'[11] This is happening today and is precisely the reason for the so-called 'occult explosion' taking place worldwide. This renewed interest in learning of the Secret Tradition is, perhaps, as once described by W.B. Yeats, a 'constant obsession for mystical rites designed to reconnect us with the natural beauty of the world, the realms of the spirits, and our own divinity'. Within the character of Merlin we find an embodiment of the qualities and knowledge necessary to reach this goal. In him we find personality and soul energies that range from the grotesque to the awe-inspiring, from the impish to the most magically skilful. Within the Merlin/magician archetype we find the urge to discover the beauty and power in Nature, and communion and harmony with the spirit forces. In doing so, we gain knowledge of our true selves. We learn that we need not look beyond or outside our own inner terrain for answers or for truth. In Tolstoy's words:

> *The wizard's enchantments have secured him a permanent place, it seems, in the consciousness of mankind. The centuries come and go, literary fashions pass, but the magician reappears before us: shifting his shape and changing his name, now mocking, now awe-inspiring, but essentially the same character whose fame flew over all Europe eight centuries ago. Trickster, illusionist, philosopher and sorcerer, he represents an archetype to which the race turns for guidance and protection.* [12]

References

1. *The Prophetic Vision of Merlin*: R.J. Stewart.
2. *The Elements of the Arthurian Tradition*: John Matthews.
3. Notably the trilogy *Taliesin, Merlin, Arthur*: Stephen Lawhead.
4. *The Landscape of King Arthur*: Geoffrey Ashe.
5. *The Quest for Merlin*: Nikolai Tolstoy.
6. Stewart, op. cit.
7. *The Secret Tradition in Arthurian Legend*: Gareth Knight.
8. Ashe, op. cit.
9. Ibid.

10. *The Hero Within*: Carol S. Pearson.
11. Tolstoy, op. cit.
12. Ibid.

THE ROUND TABLE
Medieval Medicine Wheel

The contemplation of the well-known (and not so well-known) stories of the knights and ladies of the Round Table is also one of the paths to that great inner plane Temple wherein the mightiest loving guides of the human race and the planet Earth await the questing soul.

GARETH KNIGHT

The Round Table was at the centre of King Arthur's court. One can only imagine what a huge and magnificent piece of furniture it must have been. Perhaps made from oak, it would have stood strong and stately in the middle of the great stone hall of the castle at Camelot. The walls of the hall would have been adorned with colourful banners embroidered with the different insignias of the realms within the kingdom and illuminated by the light of a huge fire that would have warmed the cold stones till they gave off a gentle heat. Around the great table the knights and ladies of the court would come together for dining and socializing. The king and his warriors would discuss battle strategies and gather around the table to celebrate the spoils of war and the victories of peace.

Although the stories of the origin of the Round Table vary, it is most often credited to Merlin, who allegedly had it made for Uther Pendragon in honour of the Last Supper. Its shape was intentionally designed to symbolize 'the roundness of the world'. When Uther died the table was passed on to King Leodegrance, a Cornish chieftain who was the father of Guinevere, and ended up at Arthur's court as part of Guinevere's dowry. Other versions of the Round Table's origins relate how the shape of the table was suggested to Arthur as a means of keeping down the jealous squabbles between his warriors. All would sit in equality at a round table. It has also been suggested that the table could be disassembled so that it might be taken wherever the king had to go on progress. Of course, when King Arthur created the Fellowship of the Knights, dedicated to upholding the high ideals of chivalry, he called it the Order of the Knights of the *Round Table*. The Jersey writer, Wace, writes:

> *On account of his noble barons, each of whom thought himself the best and none of whom accounted himself the worst, Arthur made the Round Table, of which the Britons tell many fabulous tales. There sat his vassals, all noble and all equal; they sat equally at table and were equally served. No one of them could boast of sitting higher than his peer.* [1]

But no matter where it came from or whose idea it was, from both a practical and psychological perspective, the creation of the Round Table was a stroke of genius. It allowed Arthur not only to create the climate of equality necessary for keeping the knights' egos in check but along with the equality came the unity that allowed the very existence of the Fellowship. The Round Table formed the hub of it all – a wooden focal point that embodied moral and ethical principles that were, and are, crucial to the unfolding of the human drama.

The Round Table had one vacant seat. It was called the *Siège Perilous*, the Perilous Seat, and could be occupied only by a knight who was destined for success in the search for the Holy Grail. Geoffrey Ashe tells us:

> . . . *this turned out to be Galahad, whom Pelles had tricked Lancelot into begetting, so that the Grail-achiever would be born of Joseph's stock. When Galahad arrived at the court, his vocation was shown by signs, one of them being his sitting down without mishap in the Perilous Seat.* [2]

The Joseph mentioned by Ashe is Joseph of Arimathea, who will be discussed at length in relation to the Holy Grail. Suffice it to say here that being related to the Round Table, albeit indirectly, linked Joseph with Arthur and Arthur with Christ, giving him a special spiritual image that elevated him in the eyes and hearts of the people. In any case, because the Fellowship of the Knights played such an integral role in the body of the Arthurian legends it is necessary to explore it carefully.

The Order of the Knights of the Round Table was made up of men of renown whose egos were as strong as their warring capabilities and who were on a Christian 'mission' to establish an ideal society on Earth, 'as it is in Heaven'. Throughout the legends each knight embodies both a human life and an *archetype* filled with examples of obstacles to be overcome, battles to be won, honour to be upheld, and lessons to be learned.

Most likely, training for knighthood took place in stages, reminiscent of the stages of knowledge and personal growth necessary for membership in any Mystery School or secret order or society up until present times. Gareth Knight states that:

An initiation ritual is the concentration into a small compass, in symbolic form, of the tasks that are to be performed by the soul in its evolutionary journey. It is thus a device for orienting the direction of endeavour in pictorial language that speaks to the soul. [3]

Perhaps the earliest of the stages of knightly training at the Arthurian court involved the development of physical skills and prowess that included learning to ride a horse with precision, fencing, running and foot racing, jousting, wrestling and archery. Time would have most likely been spent learning academic and esoteric disciplines such as reading and writing, astronomy and astrology, herbal lore, and knowledge of the Otherworld and Nature spirits, as well as techniques for the development of clairvoyance and other psychic skills. Likewise, proper social behaviour and the arts of dancing and making music would have been learned so as to refine the manners of the young knight and make him effective in his communication with others, especially with the lady of his choice whom he was bound to serve, protect and respect. By the time the trainee had reached the age of 21, his instruction would have reached completion and he would be ready to receive his knightly initiation.

I have oftentimes imagined that there was a special ceremony for the public during which the entire court would join in celebrating the new knights. Part of this ritual, the Ritual of the Seven Chalices, is given in the Epilogue. In my personal vision, upon acceptance into the knighthood, the new knight would be presented with his tools: a shield, helmet, mail coat, gauntlet and visor, lance and sword. Dressed in white, the neophyte would be brought into the company of the initiator and questioned as to his reasons for becoming a knight. Then, kneeling before the initiator, the candidate would be given the accolade, which consisted of being touched three times with the flat of a sword, once on either shoulder and once on the head. The blessing given might have been, as Corrine Heline suggests, 'In the name of God, St Michael, and St George, I make thee a knight; be valiant, courteous and loyal.'[4]

From that moment on, the young knight would set out to prove himself, living a life of forever being challenged and tested. A knight sought to develop nerves of steel. He sought admiration from other knights, and the affection and approval of his chosen lady. He helped those less fortunate than himself and righted wrongs whenever he could. He took chances and encountered dangers in many forms, and although his fears may have been great, his objective was always to overcome the hazards and cheat death so that he would survive to make the world a better place. Perhaps his greatest fear was that he would bring dishonour upon himself and/or his king. Because of this he would take untold personal risks to achieve his ideals. In overcoming dangers the knight would discover something of his true self.

The perils confronted by the Arthurian knights represent those that we, as individuals, must also face and overcome in order to know ourselves better and firmly establish the integrity of our own character. This is not easy, but it guarantees that each of us will be worthy to take our rightful place at 'the ultimate grand spiritual pattern of the cosmic Round Table'.[5]

Once the Fellowship of the Knights exploded upon the

scene, certain knights comprised an 'inner circle', and it is from these that we learn the most. They include Lancelot, Agravain, Gawain, Gaheris, Gareth, Kay, Tristram, Perceval, Lamorak, and, of course, King Arthur himself. Although we hear little about some of these characters, we can learn a great deal from what we do know. We also need to remember that different writers portrayed the various knights from their own perspectives so that there is often a multi-faceted identity, and even contradictory personality traits, for each of them. I have stayed as closely as possible here to those attributes that are most familiar to the general reader.

To begin with, from *Lancelot* we learn of the conflicts that come from being torn between our heart and our head, between our feelings and what our mind tells us is right. Lancelot also teaches us the difficult lessons of love and betrayal.

Through *Perceval* we learn of the dangers of having too little knowledge and experience for the challenges we must meet. We learn of the perils of impulse and the fear that comes from a dependency on others as to the actions we should or should not take.

Gareth, sometimes considered the same character as Gaheris, is given the special name of *Beaumains* by Malory, which is sometimes translated as 'generosity', and sometimes as 'fair hands'. Gareth is constantly ridiculed by Kay and he suffers interference in his love life from his lady's jealous and disapproving sister. Eventually he is accidentally killed by Lancelot in a skirmish designed to rescue Guinevere. It was Gareth's regrettable death that precipitated the conflict that was to play a major role in bringing down the Round Table. Gareth's life, on the surface, was filled with misfortunes that were not totally of his own making. However, perhaps due to his deep sense of self-worth and the fact that he never gave in to what must have been discouraging circumstances,

Gareth was not without achievement and success. He won his lady, he became a knight, and he was not forgotten in his untimely death. Gareth helps us to learn the lesson of perseverance in the face of whatever tests life may bring – to do our best, nothing more and nothing less.

Next, there is *Gawain*. As the son of King Lot and Morgause, Arthur's half-sister, he enjoyed a special relationship with Arthur and was the likely heir to the throne. For some, this would have been cause enough to search for ways to push Arthur aside and to take the kingship for himself. Rather than do this, however, Gawain made himself a valuable asset to the king. He assisted him in battle and even functioned as his special advisor. Gawain is portrayed in the legends as a champion of chivalry and peace rather than war. I see this as indicative of his high sense of morality and sensitivity and humanitarianism, although some might consider it a blind adherence to custom. While I think we have to be careful of such blindness, once we commit ourselves to a particular view or person or action, we have to be able to resist being swayed by the criticism we may receive for our commitment.

Another of Gawain's characteristics noted by most writers concerns his apparent weakness for the opposite sex. Much mention is made of his frivolous love affairs. Not only would this have gone against the code of chivalry but it would have also flown in the face of the value placed on, and the price paid for, 'real' love by some of the knights – such as Lancelot in his love for Guinevere and Arthur, too, in his love for his queen. Trouble almost always results when we play with the feelings of others, as is the case with trivial involvements. We must come to realize the value of love and not confuse it with lust or use it as the basis for purely physical or even emotional pleasures. We have to work at making certain that our attractions have merit, whether they be attractions to another person, a cause, a spiritual path, or anything else to which we give of our feelings, efforts and time.

Agravain, in league with the evil Mordred, Arthur's bastard son by either Morgause, in the earlier texts, or Morgan le Fay, in modern versions, is the knight who becomes the revealer of the secret love between Lancelot and Guinevere. It would be too easy simply to dismiss Agravain's actions as *right* because the adulterous affair was harmful to the sanctity of the Round Table and hurtful to Arthur, or as *wrong* because such a revelation should have been the sole responsibility of those involved. Rather, I think we can learn more from this character if we remember that it is perhaps always best to learn to rely on the depth of our intuition to know when to speak and when to keep silent. While it is anyone's guess as to the true motives behind Agravain's actions, I think it is safe to assume that such revelations are most often self-serving. Certainly this was clearly the case with Mordred's involvement.

In an earlier chapter we encountered *Kay*, son of Sir Ector, who was raised as Arthur's sibling. At the event of the pulling of the sword from the stone, it was Kay who at first tried to claim that it was he who had extracted it. From this we learn that we must succeed or fail by our own merit and not that of others. We cannot claim rewards that rightfully belong to others. In later adventures we see Kay being favoured by Arthur and using that favour to enter into pursuits beyond his capability. On one occasion he is allowed to go after Guinevere's kidnappers, a task in which he suffers failure and humiliation. When we look closely we discover that Kay is little more than an 'imitator'. And having a role model is one thing but mimicry is quite another! In modern works of fiction, Kay is portrayed as a fierce and angry warrior who drinks too much alcohol. Such behaviour, quite apart from the obvious perils involved, would have been at odds with the courtly society of Arthur's time and would have endangered both Kay himself and others who had to fight alongside him. So he provides us with a good example of how we behave when we are spoiled, self-centred and out of control, and when we allow ourselves to mimic others and have no vision of our own.

Finally, from *Galahad* we come to know the value of purity of mind and heart and of the nature of reaching our ultimate goal of spiritual attainment. In a later chapter I will enter into a more detailed investigation of both Lancelot and Galahad. From this overview of some of the major knights, however, we can clearly detect the 'path' of initiation embodied within the Round Table and the knights that comprised its glorious fellowship.

The personal quest is, however, but one of the mysteries embodied in the Round Table. Another, touched upon earlier, may be found in its *shape*: that of the *circle* itself. Exploration of this most ancient of symbols reveals its having long been representative of a wide range of 'powers' or 'energies' as well as certain spiritual concepts and cosmic truths. In H.P. Blavatsky's 'Proem' to *The Secret Doctrine*, Vol.I, the circle is defined as a 'plain disc' which is said to symbolize and contain 'abstract space' and the periodical manifestation of 'the ever-eternal nature'. By this definition, that which resides *within* the circle is *manifest* or physical or, at the very least, is the *potential* of all that can and will *become* manifest. All that resides *outside* the circle is *unmanifested*. Similarly, we see some of the same principles in the ancient science of Numerology, in which the circle of zero represents infinity – which has no beginning and no end. The zero is the *source* of all life and form and, at the end of the life of the physical universe, all life will be reabsorbed into it. In the Theosophical works of Alice A. Bailey and her inner plane teacher, the Tibetan, the circle is called the 'Ring Pass Not', within which all resides and evolves and beyond which none that is physical may go. Again, in the words of Native American author and literary critic, Paula Gunn Allen, the circle is '[the] concept of singular unity that is dynamic and encompassing, including all that is contained in its most essential aspects, that of life'. [6]

These definitions are admittedly deeply esoteric and universal in their implications. But when we bring the attributes of the circle down to a purely individual, personal level, we find that it has long been recognized and often used for ceremonial purposes due to its special psychic qualities. This use requires the practitioner to draw a real or imaginary circle around him or herself, usually with the aid of a magical tool such as a sword, wand or athame. The interior of the circle then becomes hallowed ground, blessed and secure, wherein the operator may indulge in invocations and rituals designed to put him in contact with spirits and natural forces who will be honoured by the magician and/or who will aid him in achieving his objectives. The circle also provides protection for the operator from outside influences and interferences, real or imagined. Furthermore, the magical practitioner understands that the circle serves yet another role in ceremonialism in that it, in and of itself, is a sort of 'generator' of energy. Energy moves in spirals, and the circle, by capturing the energy it generates, transforms it into a vortex of intense power. Wiccan rituals are known to require the construction of a circle for such uses, as are the ceremonials of most magical orders.

Additional evidence of the effectiveness of the circle as a generator of power is found in the sacred knowledge and intent inherent in the domestic architecture and ceremonial structures of the American Indian. First, let us consider the ancient 'Medicine Wheels' that dot the North American landscape in western Canada and the Great Plains of the United States. So named in indication of their assumed spiritual uses and implications and because of their circular shape, Medicine Wheels are large stone circles with inner spoke-like lines laid out with field stones on the surface of the ground. The true purpose of the ancient Wheels remains a mystery, not unlike the megalithic circles of the British Isles. Most authorities agree, however, that they were used for ceremonies as well as serving as calendars, for many of them are found to be aligned to solstice and equinox times, both of which were important spiritually and in marking the time for planting and harvesting.

More often than not, within the diverse Native American culture, we find that dwellings are also circular by design. Tipis, wigwams, igloos, hogans and most earth lodges are all round in shape with an opening left at the eastern side to let in the first light of each new dawn. To the Indian the circle is the great 'hoop' of life, the *source* of all, which symbolizes the Great Spirit and the *cycles* in Nature: birth and death, day and night, summer and winter, planting and harvest. Living within 'the Sacred Hoop' helps maintain the peoples' connection with the life energy of the universe and generates a power that promotes good heath and well-being. Sun Bear, the well-known Chippewa medicine man and teacher, tells us that life, to the Native American, is 'a Sacred Circle that takes us from birth to death to regeneration. The Native people knew how to acknowledge and celebrate the circles of their own lives, so that they were able to flow and change with the changing energies that came to them at different ages. They knew that they, like the seasons, were always moving around the Medicine Wheel, the wheel of time.'[7] At the Bear Tribe, an inter-racial medicine society formed in the late sixties by Sun Bear, the importance of the circle is taught, and is put into practice several times throughout the day. 'When we pray in the morning and evenings, we come together in a circle. Before eating, we join hands in a circle. Before sweating [a rite of cleansing] we gather in a circle. When we council, we sit in a circle.'[8]

It is for the same reasons that most Native American ceremonial lodges are also circular in design. These include the Sweat Lodge, built first by the Plains tribes as a place for prayer and for conducting a powerful cleansing rite, and the Sun Dance Lodge, for the purpose of housing an annual dance to honour the Great Mystery and to heal the sick. Also, certain sacred objects, such as the bowl of the sacred pipe and the drum used by Indians in the ceremonies, are circular in shape. Paula Gunn Allen tells us that the circle has deep implications that involve a completely different view of reality from that held by non-Indian people. She explains that Indians have a tendency to 'view space as spherical and time as cyclical'. This concept requires that all 'points' that make up the sphere of being have a specific and significant identity and purpose, whereas a linear view of time and space assumes that some 'points' are more important than others. The result is that the Indian's universe 'moves and breathes continuously, and the Western universe is fixed and static'.[9] We can safely assume that this perspective of the circle has been known and honoured by Indian tribes and others who have inherited the ancient Atlantean teachings since the earliest times, for we see by way of archaeological investigation that the circle was employed by prehistoric North Americans in petroglyphs and pictographs found on the walls of caves and cliffs, and on rocks. Most often such circles etched on stone were used to depict the sun and the full moon.

For the purpose of helping to make the circle more personal to the reader, let us return to the Medicine Wheel. As a ceremonial tool among Indian and non-Indian people today, the

Medicine Wheel is constructed first and foremost for the purpose of acknowledging the Creator as the source of all cosmic forces, which are all 'powers' and 'energies' that give birth to and sustain life in all its forms. Secondly, its ceremonial use helps the individual to make contact with the Creator and to gain entrance into the world of spirits – the Otherworld of Arthur's time – and to establish a balanced and harmonious relationship between him or herself, the Creator, and the universe.

The actual building of the Wheel involves the selection of stones – a ceremony in and of itself – which are then placed on the ground or, on some occasions, on a flat surface chosen for an indoor altar. First, at the place chosen for the centre, a stone which represents the Great Spirit is put down. Then three additional stones are placed at the centre in honour of the sun, called 'Grandfather' by the Indians, the moon, known as 'Grandmother', and the Earth Mother. The number of stones placed and what they represent and honour may vary among different tribes. But when the centre is complete, stones are always placed at a distance from the centre stones in each of the four directions to donor the four Spirit Keepers who oversee and protect the manifested universe. The four Spirit Keepers are represented by animal totems: the East by the eagle, South by the coyote, West by the bear, and North by the white buffalo. These totems may, however, also differ from tribe to tribe. The rim of the circle is then formed, creating a great hoop within which people may gather to make special prayers and to perform ceremonies to align themselves with the power that such special circles can generate and attract. Sun Bear, who has designed a unique and dynamic version of the age-old medicine hoop, teaches that in order to participate in the true lessons of the Medicine Wheel, we must remember that it is ever changing and that, although we are born at a certain station upon it, we are always travelling around it, moving from lesson to lesson, experience to experience, always gaining awareness and understanding of the powers, responsibilities and gifts inherent within each stone or station.

Such is also the spiritual nature of the Round Table. The stones of the Medicine Wheel become the members of the Fellowship of the Knights and, as we have seen, each knight embodies various human qualities, principles and challenges that represent lessons we must each learn, experiences we must each undergo, during our earthly lives.

In the same manner, the stations on the Medicine Wheel teach us and serve as a guideline for greater understanding of human nature and potential. The following is a basic overview of the 12 stones on the Medicine Wheel's outer rim according to the teachings of Sun Bear. The stones begin in the East and move in a clockwise direction around the wheel. They correspond to the 12 signs of the zodiac. The sign under which one is born holds certain lessons, as do each of the signs which are experienced as one moves from stone to stone throughout life. More detailed information on this may be gained from Sun Bear's book *Earth Astrology*.[10]

Totem:
1. Red Hawk
2. Beaver
3. Deer
4. Flicker (Woodpecker)
5. Sturgeon
6. Bear
7. Raven
8. Serpent
9. Elk
10. Snow Goose

11. Otter
12. Cougar

Corresponding Constellation:

1. Aries
2. Taurus
3. Gemini
4. Cancer
5. Leo
6. Virgo
7. Libra
8. Scorpio
9. Sagittarius
10. Capricorn
11. Aquarius
12. Pisces

Lesson:

1. Proper use of will and energy, patience, stability.
2. Overcoming over-indulgence, stubbornness.
3. Consistency, continuity, becoming less suspicious.
4. Independence, becoming less changeable, exercising emotional control.
5. Experiencing dominance, controlling the ego, arrogance.
6. Finding sympathy, becoming less critical, learning to enjoy life.
7. Exercising responsibility, becoming less gullible.
8. Becoming less swift to strike, more trusting.
9. Becoming more giving, more understanding.
10. Learning humility.
11. Turning dreams into reality, becoming adaptable
12. Gaining a greater sense of reality, emotional stability.

The reader is encouraged to work with building a personal

Medicine Wheel and to begin to experience the power of the sacred circle.

Aside from the Medicine Wheel, stone circles, some of which are extremely ancient in origin, have been erected throughout the world and, like the Medicine Wheel, their exact purposes remain unknown. It is assumed, however, that they too served both a calendric and a ceremonial need, although it is the calendric purpose that has been given the most attention, primarily by the scientific community. Recent investigations of Stonehenge, for example, have revealed much information that indicates the alignment of the structure to certain stars and/or constellations, as well as to the time of the Summer Solstice when the sun rises directly over the so-called 'heel' stone located outside the inner circle. I have come to feel personally, however, that the feature of the celestial alignments common to ancient stone circles throughout the world, including the Medicine Wheels, involves far more than simple calendric indications.

Since 1977 I have been an avid student of astronomy. A large portion of that time has been spent in investigation of what the ancient people knew about the stars, how that knowledge may have been gained, and what their relationship with the heavens meant to them. Through this study, I have gained a broader knowledge of astronomy itself and also a great deal of information about the spiritual beliefs and practices of the ancient people, along with a better understanding of the ancient mind. Our ancestors were skywatchers who found the heavens a source of wonder and mystery which they sought to understand. It is difficult, at best, for us in modern times to get a clear understanding of the impact the skies had on the consciousness of prehistoric people. In *Early Man and the Cosmos*, Evan Hadingham writes:

The sky vision shaped many aspects of their lives. It inspired stories of the world's creation and the emergence of humanity on earth. It produced a very different attitude to the passage of time from our own, driven as we are by precise clocks and calendars. The sun and stars offered a rhythm for the annual cycle of hunting and planting, and for the proper staging of religious ceremonies. The appearance of stars and planets suggested the existence of superhuman sky beings who were often associated with the power of chiefs and priests on earth, justifying the status and authority of such people.

Hadingham gets to the real crux of the matter when he notes that in the sky vision of the ancients the order of all the affairs of mankind was linked to the forces of Nature. I also agree with Hadingham when he concludes that the astrology of today is but a 'pale remnant' of the relationship once shared by man and the stars.

Earlier I made reference to Merlin's intention that the shape of the Round Table should be symbolic of the roundness of the world. In *The Landscape of King Arthur*, Geoffrey Ashe offers an interesting view on this: 'Also its shape is an image of the round world and heavens.' By turning to the *heavens* for answers concerning the forces involved in the Round Table, both as an embodiment of the energies inherent in the mystical circle and as the focal point in the illustrious Order of the Knights, we find some interesting revelations that lead to the recognition that the Arthurian epic was first written in the stars! This also adds an intriguing astronomical ingredient necessary to gaining a more complete esoteric understanding of the Matter of Britain. The first indication of there being an astronomical or celestial source for the Round Table comes from the occult writers who have said that it has its origins in the zodiac. Let me explain.

A belt that seems to encircle the Earth, the zodiac includes the 12 constellations through which the sun, when viewed from our own planetary perspective, moves on its yearly trek around us. All the other planets in the solar system follow this celestial 'circle' closely, constantly moving against the backdrop of the skies in bright and silent splendour. Each of the constellations embodies a 'force' that affects the lives and consciousness of life on Earth. While this is a definition of astrology, I prefer to think of this process of energy release as 'esoteric astronomy', and that it involves the cyclic ebb and flow of celestial powers that stimulate, perpetuate and challenge terrestrial life and affairs. The 12 forces within the zodiacal constellations are triggered into transmitting their power to the Earth by the passage of the sun and the other planets, time after time, year after year, age after age. By and through these influences, challenges are set up for mankind, the crown jewel of the lives on the Earth Mother, to meet and overcome. It is these experiences, life after life, that fuel the ever unfolding scheme of human evolution on all levels, ranging from the purely physical to the spiritual achievement of Enlightenment. We must keep in mind that although the energies of the zodiac and other constellations may indeed influence earthly life, the deepest implications that are manifested in the symbolism of the Round Table concern the forces that are more universal in nature and that are involved with the *universal* evolution of *consciousness* rather than only that which involves form or matter on Earth.

Mention of the zodiac occurs throughout the Arthurian myths, including those found in *The Mabinogion*, and were, in turn, preserved by the Druids. Their star lore is a clue that the zodiac may well be the key to the obscurities in Celtic literature, a key that will unlock the doors to many secrets within the arcane tradition that have been lost for centuries. The *Queste del San Graal* says: 'The Round Table was constructed, not without great significance, upon the advice of Merlin. By its name it is meant to signify the round world and round canopy of the planets and the elements in the firmament, where are to be seen the stars and many other things.' Thus, within the mysteries of the zodiac can be found the deepest of occult secrets of the Round Table.

Intriguing evidence pertaining to the importance of the zodiac to the archetypal mind of the ancient Briton has been discovered in the landscape surrounding the town of Glastonbury, England. Known as the Glastonbury Zodiac to some and the Temple of the Stars to others, a terrestrial circle composed of giant earth effigies has been carved into the Somerset terrain, so large that it can only be seen from above. In the book *The Glastonbury Zodiac: Key to the Mysteries of Britain*, Mary Caine describes the astonishing discovery by Katherine Maltwood, a writer and sculptor, who, in the early 1900s, while sitting on the Glastonbury Tor, rediscovered 'the ancient mystical heritage of her own country'. Caine describes the discovery as natural effigies 'moulded by hills and lesser contours, part-outlined by rivers and streams, whose course is determined by them – the whole complex measuring some ten or twelve miles across, thirty miles round . . .hardly the unaided work of man'.

Evidence of Caine's understanding of the esoteric origins of the earthly star belt is revealed when she states her belief that the zodiac was 'carved by a vaster hand; whether we like to call it Nature, Cosmic Forces, or simply God'. One can only assume it was meant to carve, with the help of the natural terrain, the star lore of the ages which forms the foundation of all traditional occult teachings in physical form upon the body of the Earth Mother herself, knowing that she would preserve what mankind would all but forget and would allow to slip into the obscurity of the depths of his unconscious mind.

Perhaps the rediscovery of the Glastonbury Star Temple is more timely than it may first appear. As we have moved closer toward jeopardizing our own survival and that of the planet, it seems as if, of their own accord, the old wisdoms have begun to return. As if a veil has been lifted, we have been witnessing this 'return', meaning acceptance and popularity amongst the masses of teachings concerning recognizing and understanding the forces of Nature, and of ceremonies that have to do with honouring and living in harmony with spirit forces, and that teach us the wisdom of choosing between black and white magic in our use of individual and collective human power. In this rebirth of interest, as has already been noted, particularly in the shamanic teachings, we seem to be groping for the old values and traditions that lie at the foundation of our unconscious and that form some of the most ancient archetypes that drive human destiny. We are becoming more ecologically aware. We are starting to realize that we must take responsibility for our own spiritual nourishment and psychological needs and, to a certain extent, even our physiological well-being. By all of this, and more, I think we can safely determine that the time has come, once again, for us to 'remember' what we have forgotten; so that we may return to the very roots of our spiritual tradition for guidance in times of global peril. The 'timing' of the return of the ancient ways and teachings is no accident. It is happening now because of our need. We must not go any further in discarding Nature. Rather, we must come once again to live in harmony with it. And we can celebrate our renewed access to paths of initiation that have been preserved for us in the Mysteries, Christian and pagan alike, in these times of spiritual famine.

In addition to the Round Table's relationship to the zodiac, there are other Arthurian star connections. Stellar constellations, while they may seem to be nothing more than arbitrary patterns in the night sky that rarely appear to form the shape of the animal or object after which they are named, are actually harbingers of 'forces' that hold deep cosmic significance and that embody powerful heavenly influences that pour energies of various types upon the Earth. An understanding of this process as an integral part of the wisdom teachings opens an entirely new perspective of the universe, the Earth, and our role as evolving humans in the scheme of it all.

Ursa Major, the constellation commonly known as the Great Bear, has also been called 'Arthur's Wain' or 'Arthur's Chariot'. The seven stars in Ursa Major have been considered by some to symbolize the Round Table and the ideals of the Order of the Knights. There is also Crater, the Cup, which embodies the power of the Holy Grail. Interestingly, one of the oldest known legends of the origin of the Grail tells of a *heavenly* battle between the Archangel Michael and Lucifer. When Lucifer was cast out from Heaven, an illustrious emerald fell from his crown into the abyss. The colour green is often associated with wisdom and its falling into the abyss most likely indicates the wisdoms coming to the physical world. The wisdoms were embodied within the Grail. (The emerald was not the only star in Lucifer's crown. The crown jewel itself was said to have been the Morning Star, considered by some to be the planet Venus and by others the planet Mercury.) The wisdom of the Grail must be earned. It cannot be possessed by the unclean of mind and heart. This means that the ego must be tamed so that the soul can come forth, for only the soul may partake of the Grail fruits.

Other celestial references can be found in Allen Artos'

book *Arthur: The King of Light.* He mentions the star Arcturus in the constellation Bootes, which was referred to in the late 1300s as Arthurus, the Warrior, and the star Capella in Auriga, the Charioteer, which in its Arabic form is the Ibex, 'Badan'. Artos asks: 'Could this be the lost Mt. Badon, the greatest of Arthur's battles? Other Arthurian battles include fighting with a giant (Orion?), a dragon (Draco?), and a bear (Ursa Major?) Perhaps each of Arthur's battles has been located in the sky as part of the hero epic.' The Draco constellation may also be related to the horned gods of primitive times, an example being Cernunnos, the stag god of the Celts. From the Christian perspective, Draco loses its position as a representative of the male god and becomes the dragon which embodies all the evil forces in mankind and which must be slain so that virtue may reign supreme. The image of St George slaying the dragon is evidence of this conversion.

The suggestion that the Mysteries have been written in the stars must be followed by the thought that they came from the stars to begin with, meaning that the stars and other celestial bodies served as portents to the ancient minds that revealed events yet to come. In this way the constellations serve the purpose of 'focusing' energies that are a major force behind the evolution of life on our planet. This is why shamans down through history have had a special knowledge of the heavens and have timed their ceremonies to correspond to the appearance of certain stars and constellations so as to 'tap' into the power inherent within them. Without doubt, average humanity has lost this celestial 'connection' just as surely as it has lost the 'connection' to Mother Earth. Throughout pagan cultures the two are found together, as in the Native American concept of Mother Earth-Father Sky. We must rediscover these relationships and come into balance with them. The path of initiation will ultimately lead us to 'reconnect' with the archetypal stars inside ourselves. Earth, sun, moon, star, air, fire and water comprise our most primitive archetypal inhabitants.

The Round Table was doomed to failure. This saddens us. We may say that it was Lancelot and Guinevere's betrayal of Arthur that tore the kingdom apart. But that betrayal, the couple's ethics, and the overwhelming passions of their emotions that caused them to disregard all reason are within each of us. Or perhaps we choose to lay the blame on the evil Mordred. But he only embodies the evil within Arthur himself, for he was born of Arthur's loins and he is, in turn, the evil capacity within each of us. No matter how many versions of the Round Table's end one may investigate, the results are always the same: in the end, the Round Table falls from the realms of fantasy and legend into the real world, where human egoic nature reigns over the path of evolution. Greed, jealousy, pride, the struggle for power and other human emotions brought the Fellowship of Knights to a tragic demise. Perhaps that was the greatest error that Arthur made in his establishment of the Fellowship: he did not take human emotion into full enough account.

How many of us, too, suffer from our idealism. How often do we try to live in a world of our own making rather than the real one. How often we go through life trying to fit square pegs into round holes. How often we try to have others conform to our image of them and seek to change them and reality to suit ourselves. These are some of the many pitfalls of idealism that we have to understand. Arthur may have failed but his failures show us what we must avoid and what we have to overcome. This makes the Round Table a blue-print for us in modern times for personal and group development. Author Richard Cavendish puts it quite eloquently:

Tales of Arthur and his knights have continued to impress and inspire long after the disappearance of the world in which they are set. Their setting, in a deeper sense, is not the Middle Ages but the world in which each of us makes the journey from birth to death. Their jousts and combats and valorous adventures are metaphors for all the struggles and battles of life.[10]

The Round Table's teaching involves learning the lessons of love, mutual respect, generosity and compassion. Until these qualities become a way of life, we will continue to fail in our quest for true fellowship with one another. Without them we cannot hope to live in true 'at-one-ment' with all life on Earth or know the brotherhood and sisterhood inherent in a respectful relationship with each other and with all that lives. The ideals we hold must not be mistaken for reality, but understood as rewards we must continue to pursue. They must be our goals and must fuel our aspirations for integrity and true self-identity, both individually and collectively. As a wheel of life the Round Table contains both the perilous elements of change and deep spiritual insights. As the archetypal *circle* it embodies all that exists. It is the Whole, the Manifested Absolute of which we are a part.

References

1. *Brut*: Wace.
2. *Mythology of the British Isles*: Geoffrey Ashe.
3. *The Secret Tradition in Arthurian Legend*: Gareth Knight.
4. *Mysteries of the Holy Grail*: Corrine Heline.
5. Knight, op. cit.
6. *The Sacred Hoop*: Paula Gunn Allen.
7. *The Path of Power*: Sun Bear, Wabun, Barry Weinstock.
8. *The Self-Reliance Book*: Sun Bear and Wabun.

9. Gunn Allen, op. cit.
10. *Medicine Wheel: Earth Astrology*: Sun Bear and Wabun.
11. *King Arthur and the Grail*: Richard Cavendish.

LANCELOT
The Flower of Chivalry

*Ah, Lancelot . . . thou art head of all Christian knights,
and now I dare say . . . there thou liest, that thou wert
never matched of earthly knights. And thou wert the
courteoust knight that ever bare shield. And thou wert
the truest friend to thy lover that ever bestrad a horse.
And thou wert the truest lover of a sinful man that ever
struck with sword. And thou wert the goodliest person
that ever came among press of knights. And thou wert
the meekest man and the gentlest that ever ate in hall
among ladies. And thou wert the sternest knight to
thy mortal foe that ever put spear in the rest.*
SIR THOMAS MALORY, LE MORTE D'ARTHUR

*No knight was ever born of man and woman, and
no knight ever sat in a saddle, who was the equal
of this man.*
CHRÉTIEN DE TROYES, ARTHURIAN ROMANCES

Lancelot was the supreme hero of the Arthurian epic. No knight could surpass him in looks, skills, physical prowess or bravery. None other received such a degree of admiration. The description afforded him by Malory portrays him as a strong opponent, unmatched in strength and skill, one willing to fight with all the passion of a great warrior. On the other hand, an equally gentle nature is revealed in his kindness and thoughtfulness. He was a man with a keen sense of fairness and who had his ego under control, for none of the glory he brought to himself ever went to his head. Although he may have been afraid, he never allowed fear to stand in the way of defending himself or those whom he loved or respected. There is clear evidence of this in his numerous rescues of Arthur. Throughout the legends, Lancelot is at the centre, defending his king and the kingdom, the woman he loved and his fellow knights, displaying his loyalty and steadfastness in the face of incredible danger.

However, all was not perfect in Lancelot's world. He was a man torn between what he knew in his mind to be right and what he felt in his heart. His love and loyalty for Arthur and the overwhelming strain that resulted from his passion for Guinevere made him a tragic figure. In the words of Richard Cavendish in *King Arthur and the Grail*:

> . . . *the conflict between his loyalty to Arthur and his love for Arthur's wife imposes an intolerable strain on him. His affair with the queen robs him of the supreme honour of winning the Grail and in the end, when Arthur can no longer close his eyes to their liaison, pits Lancelot against the leader he loves and bring Arthur's kingdom to ruin.*

Born of King Ban of Benoic in western France, Lancelot had a splendid ancestry. His father was reputed to have been

descended from King David. This would have carried a lot
of weight in Arthur's Christian kingdom for it gave Lancelot
direct connection to Jesus the Christ. He is often referred
to in the myths as Lancelot du Lac (*du Lac* meaning 'of the
Lake'), which suggests that there were also pagan
connections in the background of the illustrious knight.
After the death of his father, the infant Lancelot was
kidnapped by the Lady of the Lake and taken into the
Otherworld where he was raised as her own son. She never
told the lad of his true identity. This, of course, is
reminiscent of Arthur's childhood, when he was taken by
Merlin to be reared as the son of Sir Ector. At the age of
18, the Lady of the Lake presented Lancelot at Arthur's court
where he flowered into the best of all the knights. At the
time of his knighting ceremony, the mother-priestess
presented Lancelot with a gift of his arms, again reminding
us of Arthur, in his reception of Excalibur.

One of the earliest of Lancelot's adventures occurred
when he broke the evil spell against Dolorous Gard, a castle
in the North. It was there that he found a tomb with his own
name inscribed upon it. Realizing the castle was his home
and would be his future grave site, Lancelot took possession
and renamed it Joyous Gard.

The love story of Lancelot and Guinevere had its origin
in Celtic mythology. While the court was at Camelot,
Guinevere was abducted and taken to the land of Gorre by
its king's wicked son, Meleagant. An unsuccessful attempt
was made to free her by the knight Kay, but he too was
captured and imprisoned. This led Lancelot and Gawain to
set out to rescue them both. Along the way, Lancelot
encountered a dwarf who offered to assist the knight in his
search if he would but climb onto the cart he was driving.
Lancelot was reluctant, for to ride in the cart would have
been a sign of weakness, for only convicted criminals rode

in such vehicles. But, after taking only two steps, his love for Guinevere overcame him and he gave in. Gawain refused to join Lancelot in the cart.

After overcoming several diversions and tests designed to thwart his quest, Lancelot crossed over the perilous Sword Bridge into the land of Gorre. Upon his later arrival, Gawain chose to enter the kingdom by the easier, but still treacherous, Underwater Bridge. When Lancelot saw Guinevere, she shunned him, later explaining to him that the two steps he took before giving in to the dwarf and climbing into the cart indicated that his knightly pride was stronger than his love for her. But after a while she relented and they spent a night of love together.

The next day Lancelot freed the members of the court who had been held captive, only to be captured himself. After finally being released, the knight returned to Camelot, vowing to kill Meleagant in a combat that would be arranged between them at Arthur's court a year later. The agreement was that should Lancelot lose the duel, Guinevere would be returned to Gorre. In the intervening time the love between Lancelot and Guinevere grew and they went to great lengths to spend time together. Lancelot would, so it seems, have done just about anything to please Guinevere, as is evidenced in one story when he agrees to play the coward during a jousting tournament!

When the day of the duel came, Meleagant was no match for Lancelot. The knight's anger had become a passion. Without mercy, Lancelot beheaded the ill-fated evil prince, much to the approval of Arthur and the court.

No doubt Lancelot knew that his feelings for Arthur's queen were sinful, and his disloyalty to his best friend and king and were by now weighing heavy on him. But, sadly, he could not overcome his passion. In fact, it was Guinevere's love for him which he credited with making him the successful knight and warrior that he was.

Guinevere was not the only woman who was attracted to Lancelot and sought to win his love. Another was Morgan le Fay. Her tactic was to convince Arthur of his queen's involvement with Lancelot. After this failed several times, Morgan resorted to magic to try and seduce the illustrious knight and win his affections for herself. One tale has her giving Lancelot a sleeping potion. When he fell asleep, she stole a precious ring that had been given to him by Guinevere. Morgan took the ring to Arthur and offered it as proof of the queen's adultery. Although anxious about how Lancelot would react, Guinevere denied any wrongdoing and Arthur believed her. Determined not to fail, Morgan then captured Lancelot and imprisoned him in her castle. While there, the knight, in his misery, drew pictures of Guinevere on the walls in his room. When shown the pictures, Arthur became suspicious, but would still not let himself accept the reality of the relationship.

The only woman other than Guinevere who was to play a meaningful role in Lancelot's life was Elaine, the beautiful virgin daughter of King Pelles. While Lancelot was visiting the king's castle, Elaine came into the great hall carrying a golden cup. Pelles wanted Elaine to bear Lancelot a son who would succeed in the quest for the Holy Grail. Lancelot was tricked into believing that the queen had sent for him and coupled with Elaine. Afterwards, realizing that he had been deceived, Lancelot was filled with anger. But he forgave Elaine when she stated that in her womb he had planted the seed of the noblest knight that would ever live. That child was to be Galahad.

Predictably, Guinevere was passionately jealous of Elaine. Though he loved only the queen, Lancelot could not absolutely convince her of this, and when she learned he had slept with Elaine as the result of yet another enchantment, she drove him away, saying that she never wanted to see him again. Lancelot went mad and retreated into the wilderness where he remained for many years. Reduced to little more than a wild animal, he eventually wandered into Corbenic where Elaine recognized him and took him into her castle home where the Holy Grail was kept. After the Grail had restored his sanity, Lancelot and Elaine retreated to Joyous Gard. Nothing, however, could soothe Lancelot's grief at the loss of Guinevere. He only agreed to return to Camelot when his brother, Ector, and the knight, Perceval, came to him. Lancelot then participated in the search for the Holy Grail but was unsuccessful. He knew that his passion for Guinevere was what prevented him from realizing the ultimate goal. His heart was not pure, his feelings a sin.

It was inevitable that Arthur would have to admit to the reality of the relationship shared by Lancelot and Guinevere and, upon doing so, he was forced by the court to condemn his unfaithful wife to death. Once again, she was rescued by Lancelot, and taken to Joyous Gard. Yet, once Arthur agreed to assure Guinevere's safety, Lancelot, true to his deep love for the king, returned Guinevere to him. But the damage was done. The Round Table split into those loyal to Arthur and those loyal to Lancelot. Consequently, Lancelot and his followers left for France, where he set up his own court.

As an individual, Lancelot had it all. He was the perfect male whom every man wishes to imitate, the archetypal 'knight in shining armour' of whom every woman dreams, the ultimate role model for the masculine human experience. But when we go beyond his physical qualities and achievements, we see a much more complex individual whose role within the Arthurian epic comprises a degree of human initiation that is equal in importance to that of Arthur himself. The key to understanding Lancelot and what lessons and challenges he shows us should be explored carefully. There is also value in seeking to unravel the esoteric and symbolic implications contained within his personality and the events that occurred in his life. Let us begin with his early life.

You will recall that upon the death of his father, Lancelot was spirited away by the Lady of the Lake. We can assume therefore that during his childhood he was versed in pagan tradition and taught the ways of the magical arts. He would have been no stranger to Avalon. It was not uncommon for legendary heroes to have been taught the ancient wisdoms and trained for battle by *women*, for such was an authentic and ancient Celtic practice. I think that two things are indicated by Lancelot's association with the Lady of the Lake. One is that Lancelot was capable of using the art of enchantment himself. He would have been a trained healer. He would have known the laws of Nature and how to function in perfect order with them. In fact we see him using his magical healing powers on numerous occasions, always for the purpose of eliminating the pain of others. He would have known of the future and with such powers, surely he knew that his love affair with Guinevere was doomed to failure and pain. And although his emotions proved stronger than his sense of what was right, we never see him using magical powers to win Guinevere for himself, to aid him in battle, or for any type of personal gain. Secondly, given that Lancelot was 'chosen' by none other that the High Priestess of Avalon herself and trained in the ancient ways, it is safe to assume that his destiny was recognized by the Lady to be one of great importance in the entire scheme of things. Perhaps he was, in some ways, a 'test' for the morality of the Christian court of Arthur.

His failure in the Grail quest, however, brought humiliation to this proud knight. And he knew, as stated earlier, exactly what had caused his failure – his heart was burdened with guilt, and only the purest of knights could look upon the Grail and claim it and its glories for himself. Also, although Lancelot was a skilful knight, strong in body, hot in temper yet controlled in his actions, by his own admission, he was *dependent* upon Guinevere's affections for him to manifest those qualities. Without Guinevere's affections we see Lancelot reduced to little more than a sad and insane figure stripped of his ability to function as a knight or live up to his priorities and values. His qualities were not *really* diminished, but he did not realize that. As far as he was concerned, without Guinevere, he was nothing. He saw nothing in himself to give and no reason to live. His own allowance of the devaluation of his self-image was the cause of Lancelot's downfall – it cost him everything he valued, including his political and brotherly alliance with Arthur.

We last hear of Lancelot when he arrives in England too late to help Arthur in his campaign against Mordred. The grieving knight learns that Guinevere has retreated to a convent at Amesbury near Salisbury Plain, taken religious vows and become a nun. Ridden with the guilt of knowing that it was her love affair that had led to the deaths of Arthur and his most gallant knights, she bids Lancelot go back to his own land and take a wife and be happy, for they must never see each other again. Lancelot is devastated by Guinevere's words and vows that he too will retreat from the world and live a life of abstinence, for he can never marry nor find happiness with anyone but her. Lancelot goes to Glastonbury and joins Sir Bedivere, who is already living there in a hermitage. Several other knights come to be with them and, some six years later, Lancelot is ordained as a priest. A year later, a message comes to the hermitage that Guinevere has died. Some versions of the myths say that

Lancelot and his companions then went to the nunnery and took her body to Glastonbury, where she was buried with Arthur. His heart broken, Lancelot then grieves to death, and his body is taken to Joyous Gard.

Through Lancelot we can confront many of life's greatest challenges. One of these involves the nature of commitment. In a psychic transmission in 1987 at Glastonbury, I was asked a vital question by my Inner Voice: 'Do you truly have an understanding of the powerful force present within *commitment*?' I realized, as I pondered the values and demands contained within the term, that we live in a society where commitment is on the wane. I thought about the marriage commitment, for one, and realized that there has to be a reason why almost half of the marriages in America fail. I thought about how vows are broken all too easily and how most of us enter into them without enough forethought as to what is really involved in making the commitment involved in marriage and other types of relationship. I thought about how often we act on the spur of the moment or on the emotions born of desire. Here we see Lancelot, torn between his vow to Arthur, his vows of chivalry and his love for Guinevere. His commitment to Arthur involved far more than political alliance. It had to do with loyalty to the sovereignty, commitment to the people and country of Britain, and with the oath taken to be a worthy member of the Fellowship of Knights and the brotherly union it embodied. All of this was pitted against what Lancelot felt in his heart – and how often are such commitments diminished by passion! When does passion empower us, as individuals, in our quest for self-knowledge? When does it become destructive and set us up for a downfall? The line is surely very thin, for passion can indeed be a strong and powerful force to be reckoned with.

Handled properly, it can be a potent personal tool that gives us the necessary power for growth and achievement; it can keep us focused on the path we have chosen for our life's purpose and work. Everything depends on our response to it and our ability to deal with that response.

Passion, be it of a positive or negative nature, plays an immense role in the way we create a fate for ourselves, and shape our view of reality. Positive passion can cause us to take actions against cruelty and injustice. It can fuel dedication and devotion. It can transform us and guide us into elevating our compassion from pity for one hungry child into an awareness of the hungry of all nations, from sympathy for one bird with a broken wing into empathy for all who are unfortunate. But we must also understand that passion has its negative qualities. Passion is as intense a power as can be. It can also be fleeting, its energy spent quickly, resulting in the kind of impulse and impatience that often leads to serious errors in judgement. As with Lancelot, passion can cause us to compromise ourselves and our ethics. We all have Lancelot within us, the knightly part of ourselves who is called upon to confront our passions and face our commitments in life.

Like Lancelot, we, too, often want what we cannot have. Lancelot allowed his desire for Guinevere to colour most of his life. It dictated his definition of success. And most importantly, it caused him to look to someone else for strength and courage and happiness. His knighthood became little more than a *persona* perceived by others, and bore little resemblance to the real human being underneath. He vacillated between being in touch with who and what he was as 'the best knight' and going insane from his feelings for Guinevere. While Lancelot cannot be completely denied his capabilities as a great warrior and hero, he falls short of the rewards he had the potential of achieving. Perhaps the saddest evidence of this is seen when, on his visit to Castle Carbonek, he paused and knelt reverently at the door of the room that held the Holy Grail. As he was about to enter the room, a voice forbade it. He was allowed only to look at the table of silver upon which rested the Sacred Cup covered with red samite, the holy cross and the other silver ornaments. He knew that he was seeing all that he would ever see of the Grail, and was blinded for his pains. Downhearted, he turned and left to return to his own country.

For the rest of his life Lancelot grieved for his loss and for the sins he had committed that had cost him any claim to the Sacred Cup. His passions had blinded him. They had caused him to live up to only a portion of his potential, as a man and as a knight. How many times do we find ourselves in Lancelot's position? How often is it too late to do anything about it or to avert the pain we have created?

The source of Lancelot's pain was his love for Guinevere, but when we really think about it, was this truly love or was it obsession? Obsession causes one to allow a particular person, thing, feeling or idea to completely dominate one's thoughts. It motivates one's actions and is a dangerous state to live in. Obsession demands *all* that we have, all time, all energy, all of our power. Nothing can overrule its force as it burns its way through every fibre of our being. It veils truth and prevents us from using what we know to be true to guide and direct our lives. Ultimately, obsession destroys. It destroyed the Fellowship of the Knights of the Round Table. It destroyed Lancelot's chances of ever achieving the Holy Grail or of partaking of its spiritual nectar. It destroyed the trust that once existed between him and Arthur. It tore apart the sacredness of the marriage of Arthur and Guinevere, denying the people a faithful queen. It divided the loyalties of the knights. It caused the pain of separation and the grief of a broken heart. And, in the end, it robbed Lancelot of even the breath of life itself. Obsessions may be far easier to fall into than to break free of. But we can learn from the dangers involved with obsession: we can learn from Lancelot and his pain.

Aside from the purely human characteristics, both positive and negative, that we see in Lancelot, there are also *archetypal* and *esoteric* qualities that bear investigation. First, as the model of the 'most perfect knight in the world', Lancelot, like Arthur, embodied both the hero and warrior archetypes. On the one hand, the hero archetype formed the basis of Lancelot's position as the most admired and beloved knight one in the court and the object of women's affections. However, the somewhat harsh edges of the warrior and the type of bravery that comes from the warrior's personality and actions also contributed to his overall behavioural patterns. Although some considerations of these two archetypes were discussed in the chapter on Arthur, let us look at them in more depth as they pertain to Lancelot, as they formed almost the total foundation of his character. First the hero.

In *The Hero Within*, Carol S. Pearson offers a clear and revealing definition of the hero when she writes: 'Heroes take journeys, confront dragons, and discover the treasure of their true selves.' In a similar manner, Joseph Campbell identifies the hero as 'the master of the world'. Both of these definitions give us some valuable insight into the real power behind this powerful archetype. They suggest that the hero does not wait for the world and its experiences to come to him. Rather, he goes out into the world to confront and 'slay the dragon' and, in doing so, combats the sense of emptiness and fear that comes from inaction. It is by and through the 'doing' that the hero learns something of himself – what his individual fears are, what his strengths and weaknesses are, and what he is capable of doing to change himself and the world around him. Lancelot did this. Typically for the hero, he not only destroyed the 'villain', in whatever form it may have taken at any given time, but he also *rescued* the victim. This more clearly distinguishes the true hero from the warrior. Through his willingness to confront the perils that threatened the court and its members, especially those involving Guinevere, he succeeded in endearing himself to others and in elevating himself to the highest level of honour and respect. He did not only use his physical skills to accomplish his heroic acts. Time and again we see Lancelot using his occult knowledge and skills to heal the afflicted or to otherwise right wrongs and to transform a person, place, or thing, adding a special charm not seen in any of the other knights. However, with Lancelot, it is very difficult to define the hero that he was without including the *warrior* as an integral part of his overall character.

Generally, a warrior is one who fights in battle. But when viewed more closely there is, perhaps, much more to it than that. First and foremost, the warrior must have a strong physical body and he must know how to use it skilfully in meeting and overcoming whatever negative obstacles he faces. But the warrior must also be a good *strategist* so that his battles are carefully planned and the right choices may be made and defended. Likewise, the warrior is committed to a 'cause' that he feels is worth fighting for. He is the defender of the faith or rights of the people or the kingdom itself. Carol Pearson states that 'This archetype helps teach us to claim our power and to assert our identity in the world.' She brilliantly points out that the warrior's actions involve the creation of acceptable 'boundaries' so that humanity knows its parameters – 'where we end and other people begin'. The warrior is not afraid to assert himself, and we can learn from him the lesson of *knowing* what is right and wrong for ourselves. In so doing, we learn *self-trust* and *self-reliance*. So often we speak boldly about what our particular views and values are, but when the time comes to defend those notions we are not always capable of doing so – or even willing. Without the willingness to stay and fight, no matter what the cost, the warrior will, ultimately, suffer from the personal tragedies of inferiority and shame. But by fighting, the warrior becomes, more often than not, the hero, one archetypal response triggering another into awakening.

Throughout his life Lancelot enjoyed the limelight of the warrior, which elevated him to the status of the hero in the eyes of the court. In the end, however, he lost the hero status when he saw that his feelings for Guinevere were an unconquerable barrier to his maintaining his prowess and position. His emotions drained his *will* and usurped his *power*. Fighting was always Lancelot's signature of personal integrity, for during conflict he was able to be most fully himself. All of himself – physically, emotionally, mentally and spiritually – was stirred into action. He deployed his battle skills – courage, fearlessness, training and experience – with precision and accuracy and a sense of intense determination and will. Such power provides a perfect opportunity for a warrior to transcend the purely physical realms of action and reach the more sublime levels experienced by the hero when he is freed from the shackles of personal inadequacy, uncertainty and fear. Thus freed, the warrior can attain what Richard Cavendish describes as 'a rapture of self-fulfilment in which he seems superhuman'. [1]

Lancelot became ashamed of the sins he committed against Arthur, the principles of Christianity and court ethics he violated. He lost the hero status and wanted to hide himself away from the eyes of his peers. As a warrior he fought purely for self-defence or for the sake of fighting out of frustration. We must remember that it was Guinevere's love and admiration that stirred Lancelot to the achievements of heroism and victory, so when he lost that he lost everything, including his self-control. So his conflict of loyalties between Arthur and the court on the one hand, and the queen on the other, resulted in failure in the most important challenge of his life, the Grail Quest. He had to go through the pain of hearing that Guinevere had suffered public ridicule and had been sentenced to die for her disloyalty to the king. And then, perhaps the most painful of all, he found himself pitted against Arthur, his beloved king and friend. He saw the Fellowship of the Round Table split into two factions. He accidentally killed Agravain and Gareth. He could not live in or deal with the everyday world once he realized that Guinevere had gone into the nunnery and so he, too, retreated into religious life – which may also have served the purpose, consciously or unconsciously, of appeasing his guilt over the ethical code he had broken. Finally he starved and grieved himself to death, a sad and pitiful end for the world's most perfect knight.

All this happened because Lancelot was the victim of an *ideal*. He had lived the life of the *ideal* man, knight, lover and warrior – and that ultimately doomed him to personal failure. Ideals die hard. Perhaps it is more correct to say that Lancelot was the man, the knight, the lover and the warrior that all thought him to be. But the damning thing was that he himself lost sight of these qualities, or the presence of them, within himself.

How many of us lose sight of ourselves in this way. The development of the warrior within may very well be essential to the recognition and unfolding of a more whole person and to the living of a full life, not only for the purpose of actually fighting on a battlefield but as a source of strength and courage that help us confront obstacles and break down personal barriers in the battleground of life. The warrior archetype gives us the qualities needed to become dedicated to a 'cause'. But we must handle it properly, for its misuse can prevent us from entering into the realm of the hero. We have to value ourselves for what we are – be that positive or negative – and separate that from what others may think us to be.

Sooner or later, too, we come to realize that being a warrior is not enough. While the warrior may have conquered enough of his fears to respond to danger and competition without hesitation, he will, as Carol Pearson states 'at some point . . . get burned out if . . . not exposed to any other way of doing things'. Her additional comments about the warrior's need to share feelings, fears and vulnerabilities with his peers and to be candid while at the same time acting on his own convictions and maintaining respect for others can go far in assuring personal success and the success of whatever groups the warrior forms a part. Lancelot hid his feelings for Guinevere. He – and she – went to great lengths to conceal the truth, which only resulted in their lives becoming a lie. In the end, this lie dealt the fatal blow, both literally and symbolically, to the ideal knight, and the warrior/hero/best knight became little more than a *persona* that concealed the real and total man that Lancelot was.

Tragically, the one thing about Lancelot that never wavered or diminished was his love for Guinevere. From this we can also learn a great and painful lesson. Such a love could have carried Lancelot to the highest of human levels just as easily as it brought him down. From this we see again how our fate is dependent upon our response to what we feel, how far we are willing to go and what sacrifices we are willing to make in order to have what we want. Lancelot could not bring himself to give up his relationship with

Arthur and his loyalties to the court. He could not break the code of chivalry by which he vowed to live. But neither could he give up Guinevere. He could not let anyone down, so to speak, and so he lost it all, drawing upon himself the very conditions and repercussions he feared.

Though bittersweet, Lancelot remains one of the most unforgettable characters in the Arthurian epic. Viewed from the perspective of the most perfect knight in the world, he becomes a role model for all to admire. Viewed negatively, he becomes the tragic figure whose love obsession cost him everything. Perhaps the real Lancelot is lost somewhere in the middle ground between the ideal knight and the tragic lover. Through his valiant experiences we can discover our level of physical power and find ways we can utilize those powers for the good of the group and the whole. Through his failings we can learn how better to cope with the obstacles on the road to self-fulfilment. Through him we can come to understand the bitterness of failure when once we tasted the sweetness of success. Thus we come to value the personal balance that can exist between these two opposites we all possess and must face.

And thou were the goodliest person that ever came among the press of knights.
ECTOR DE MARIS, BROTHER OF LANCELOT[2]

Lancelot was buried at Joyous Gard. So ended the life of the man who was portrayed in *Morte D'Arthur* as 'the one who arouses the most heartfelt sympathy and admiration'. He does so, perhaps, because he was indeed, above all, so human.

References

1. *Arthur and the Grail*: Richard Cavendish.
2. *Morte D'Arthur*: Sir Thomas Malory.

5

EXCALIBUR

Deadly Weapon or Magical Wand?

Forged in the fires of a windy night, it is invincible. Worked by the dark of the moon, it is invincible. Tempered in waters sacred to the gods, it is invincible. Risen now from the heart of the lake, it is invincible. No other blade will withstand its stroke.
PERSIA WOOLEY, *CHILD OF THE NORTHERN SPRING*

Down through time priests and priestesses of various holy orders and cultures have cherished objects they held to be sacred. These have ranged from trees to stones, from feathers to magical wands. Holy chalices have held healing waters from holy wells and springs, while sacred pipes have been lifted to the lips of shamans throughout time. Such a special object was Excalibur, the magical sword of King Arthur.

Although Excalibur is considered by some to have been the same sword that was pulled from the anvil in the stone by the youthful Arthur to reveal that he was the rightful heir to the British throne, that is not likely, for the time simply does not fit. Rather, the more popular accounts of the appearance of the illustrious Excalibur tell of Arthur, after breaking his own sword in battle, being led by Merlin to a lake. There they see a hand rising out of the water and in it is Excalibur. Merlin explains to Arthur that the sword is a gift for him from the Lady of the Lake, the powerful Enchantress of Avalon, and that it will save him from ever being inflicted with a mortal wound. Arthur is also told that the beautiful jewelled scabbard that holds the sword is even more potent and that it possesses the power of protecting its wearer from injury and bleeding. The sword should belong to Arthur alone and will protect him for the rest of his life. There is a wonderful description of the scabbard and its sword found in Persia Wooley's novel *Child of the Northern Spring*, even though the setting suggests a time before Arthur was king:

> *Behold also the sheath, enriched by my own hands with the spells of healing, that it may staunch the flow of blood for the man who wears it on his belt. Mark well this weapon's magic; from this day forth it shall be the sign of Celtic destiny, shall give witness to the integrity of its owner, shall be the symbol by which all men know the choice of the Goddess. For there is only one man for whom Excalibur was made . . . the next High King of Britain.*

The history of Excalibur is one that is filled with the kind of excitement that one expects from the adventures of King Arthur and his knights. One incident involving the famed sword concerned Arthur and his half-sister, Morgan le Fay. Morgan, portrayed as an evil enchantress in the legends, secretly hated Arthur and was jealous of him. This caused her to seek ways to destroy him. Finally she stole both sword and scabbard, and, through her magic, made false replicas of them. Later, while out on a morning hunt, Arthur chased a stag deep into the forest. In the evening, he came to a river where he sighted a ship that was completely covered with silk. As it sailed closer to him, he saw that there was no one aboard. Curiosity overcame the king and he went on board for closer inspection. Immediately, 100 torches came to light and 12 lovely maidens appeared and served the king a feast after which he retired to bed and fell into a deep sleep. Upon awakening, Arthur realized that he had fallen into a trap, for he found himself in a dungeon with 20 other knights. The ship had been sent by Morgan for her own sinister reasons. An interesting side note to this is that ships that sail by themselves are often found in the Arthurian legends and are the vessels for transporting an important person, usually a hero, to an enchanted world.

The dungeon where Arthur found himself was that of an evil lord named Damas who was involved with his brother in a land dispute. A combat was to be fought between two champions representing the brothers, and Arthur was given the opportunity to free himself, and the other knights, if he would fight for Damas. He agreed, reluctantly, for he was torn between his desire for freedom and his unease at having to fight for a wrongful cause. His rival, representing Damas' brother, was Accolon, Morgan le Fay's lover. She, unknown to anyone, had given Accolon the real Excalibur and Arthur a fake one. As expected, Arthur's sword was impotent against Excalibur and it looked as if he could not win in his fight against Accolon. Soon the battle reached such a fury that Arthur's life was in serious jeopardy. At a critical moment, however, Nimuë, the Lady of the Lake, appeared and, with her magical power, made Excalibur fly out of Accolon's hand. Arthur grabbed it and struck his rival such a strong blow that blood poured from his ears! Accolon surrendered, admitting that the entire affair had been the work of Morgan le Fay. Arthur spared his life but Accolon later died of his wounds. Arthur sent his dead body to Morgan as a gift.

This episode clearly indicates a misuse on Morgan's behalf of magical knowledge and powers – and how such misuse can indeed backfire! With the appearance of Nimuë, we not only see that not all practitioners of the magical arts have evil intentions but also that Arthur was under the protection of 'forces' that were much stronger than the sorcery of one individual. In addition, in this incident Arthur has to deal with both positive and negative feminine forces: the negative represented by Morgan and the positive by the Lady of the Lake. Although these feminine forces appear to be on the outside, they were, in truth, within Arthur himself.

Another event with Excalibur also involved Morgan: with some male companions, she succeeded in stealing the sword's magical scabbard while Arthur was sleeping. Morgan wanted to steal Excalibur too but the king was holding it tightly while he slept. When Arthur awoke and realized what had happened, he set out in hot pursuit of Morgan, who threw the scabbard into a lake. The sorceress escaped being captured by using her magical skills to transform herself and her escorts into stone statues. Seeing the statues made Arthur think that God had punished Morgan and her men for their acts. However, no sooner had Arthur left than Morgan transformed herself and her escorts into humans again and they all took refuge in one of her castles.

Here, once again, we see Arthur falling victim to the evil powers of a woman, a message that is inherent in the more Christianized versions of the myths and that was to seal the fate and reputation of women for centuries to come. Women must not be trusted, for they will rob you of your powers, as evidenced by Morgan's stealing the scabbard. Many adventures of betrayal and black magic are spread throughout the whole array of the Arthurian legends and when viewed from the metaphysical perspective, they show the imbalance between the masculine and feminine powers in Nature, in relationships, and in the use of the powers gleaned from knowledge gained from the wisdoms themselves. Oftentimes they also point out weaknesses in the human character.

At the end of Arthur's earthly life, we find him involved in a great battle against his illegitimate son, Mordred, the battle that was to seal the fate of the Order of the Round Table and end Arthur's reign. After the Grail Quest was over and many of the knights were dead or lost, Mordred had begun to plot to overthrow his father and take the throne for himself. He arranged for Lancelot and Guinevere to be discovered together in the queen's chambers so that Arthur could no longer ignore their relationship. Mordred's devilish scheme came just at the time that the beleaguered lovers had decided that they must end their affair for the good of the kingdom. Once the diabolical plot unfolded and the lovers were found out, Mordred forced Arthur to sentence Guinevere to be burned at the stake. Lancelot rescued her, but not without terrible consequences, for during the rescue he killed Gaheris and Gareth, faithful knights and servants to the king, instigating a war which not only saw the death of another knight, Gawain, but also gave Mordred the opportunity to seize the throne in his father's absence and proclaim himself king.

Upon his return, Arthur fought against his bastard son. During this battle he received the mortal wound that was to be his last – but not before he had slain the evil Mordred with his own hands, as he had sworn to do. Taken from the battlefield by Sir Bedivere, Arthur ordered the knight to take Excalibur and throw it into a nearby lake. But, thinking the sword so beautiful that he did not wish to throw it away, Bedivere hid it behind a tree and returned to his dying king. When questioned as to what he saw when he tossed Excalibur into the water, Bedivere replied that he had witnessed nothing. Arthur knew by this answer that the knight had not carried out his orders and demanded, once again, that he do so. Still reluctant, Bedivere again tried to deceive Arthur. But the king sent him a third time and finally the sword was hurled into the lake with all the knight's might. A hand came out of the waters and, seizing Excalibur, shook it three times in the air. Then, still grasping the sword, the hand sank beneath the dark waters. What had come from the Otherworld had now been reclaimed by the Otherworld.

So Excalibur, a tool that symbolized Arthur's manhood and kingship, was once more absorbed into the waters of the unconscious. The king's earthly life was over, his work done. He could now leave the physical world. Bedivere carried the king's body to the edge of the water where a barge with several women, including Morgan le Fay and the Lady of the Lake, dressed in black robes and hoods, awaited. The mourners took the body and pulled away from the shore. In exclamation of his fear, Bedivere cried out to his king, begging for the answer to what he should do now that he was left alone among his enemies. 'Comfort thyself,' replied Arthur, 'and do as well as thou mayest, for in me is no trust to trust in. For I must go into the vale of Avilion [Avalon] to heal me of my grievous wound. And if thou hear nevermore of me, pray for my soul.'[1]

As already discussed, Arthur's life reveals several important 'initiatory' experiences a human being must undergo, and in this final scene Bedivere's reluctance to cast

Excalibur into the lake can be seen to represent our own struggle with holding onto material things and values. It was only due to Arthur's insistence that Bedivere finally let go and did the right thing. As the magical sword is reclaimed by the hand in the water, we see it return to the realm of the unconscious, representative of the 'womb' from which all has come.

Morgan le Fay's role in these incidents is as the usurper of power. By taking Excalibur she attempts to take Arthur's power, the power that is the kingship and all that comes along with it. Her aim is also, more personally, to render him vulnerable and weak. Arthur was told that the jewelled scabbard was more potent than Excalibur itself. But he left it unattended and Morgan was able to steal it. This shows that we must cover everything – we cannot leave any part of ourselves open to those people or things or values that would rob us of our personal power. When Arthur received Excalibur he acquired a power with it that, when properly directed, would protect him and, subsequently, the entire kingdom. Power demands being responsible for what we know, and power, as we see time and again, must not and cannot be misused or underestimated. In the incidents where Morgan is able to steal the sword and/or the scabbard, Arthur displays a damaging lack of judgement and wanton irresponsibility.

An interesting perspective may also be gleaned from viewing Arthur's magical sword as a symbol of our own *spiritual path*. Whether we choose a particular religion or philosophy or some other form of belief and practice on which to mould our lives, there are many roads upon which we can travel to attain greater knowledge of ourselves and the universe of which we are a part. Today some follow the Native American path of power, some are Buddhists, Hindus or Moslems and some are Christians, while others choose teachings such as Eckankar, Wicca, Science of Mind or Scientology to reach the same goals. Even atheism is a path. But no matter what the belief adhered to, each one is, like Excalibur, a double-edged sword. First, the sword is held in one's own hand, for the path is one's personal choice, and so is one's fate. The straight blade of the sword is the path itself, the specific teaching and/or creed involved. One edge of the blade is that of the severity we encounter when we indulge too deeply in the physical world and its pitfalls and material values. With it comes the problems of addiction, glamour, imbalance, suffering and death. The other edge of the blade is that of idealism, with its pitfalls of illusion, wishful thinking, blind faith, spiritual immaturity, emotional indulgence and idealism itself. Both are equally destructive, though both present us with valuable lessons that must be learned. To truly walk the path, one must experience both edges, for experience is the greatest teacher, while always returning to the centre to digest the experience. To remain on either edge will defeat us.

Turning from the sword to the scabbard, Gareth Knight addresses the issue so clearly when he writes:

> The scabbard is that which contains the sword. A sword unsheathed is an awkward and dangerous object; it needs to be within its scabbard except on the rare occasion of combat, for everything a sword touches it will cut. The virile force of the spirit is similar. It needs must be contained and the scabbard therefore signifies the power, knowledge and wisdom of its containment.[2]

Here, Knight is describing the human make-up, namely the body, the scabbard, as the vehicle of 'containment' and the soul, Excalibur, as the indwelling dynamic spiritual force. Both of these parts of ourselves must be guarded with equal attention. They have to be equally nourished and sustained.

No one can live a full life only in the material realm – the force and strength of the soul has to be brought to bear on our physical existence before there can be true balance.

I would like to digress from the symbolic and spiritual attributes of Excalibur at this point and consider it purely as a sacred object that belonged to one person. In this respect, Excalibur is not unlike other such objects possessed and used by shamans up to the present day: Buddhists have their prayer beads and the sacred bell and dorje, Christians have the cross and Moslems have the sacred black stone at Mecca. Nowadays, as in the ancient past, crystals and other minerals, pipes, eagle feathers, a variety of sacred plants and the talons and claws of totem animals are objects that are used to aid the shaman in his practice of the magical arts and to draw the aspirant into closer contact with the more subtle worlds of existence. A sacred object, no matter what 'form' it may have, is a true 'companion' to its owner and is always treated with great honour and respect.

Sometimes such an object, like Excalibur and its scabbard, comes to a person as a gift. Such an object may have a history of traditional use, making it a powerfully charged sacred heirloom, or it may have been fashioned especially for the person to whom it is given, giving it a power of a different but special kind. Usually such an object has been 'charged' with energy that is meant to serve a particular purpose, such as protection or the bringing of prosperity or fertility. On the other hand a holy object may be a replica of an original as is seen in the case of the pipe of the Native Americans. The original pipe was, like Excalibur, a gift from the spirit world, in this case a gift to the Sioux Indian people from a Spirit Woman known as White Buffalo Calf Woman. All other pipes have been designed and used according to the intent of the original, which is for prayer and communication with the Creator. For the latter purpose the pipe serves as a 'link' between the physical and spiritual worlds.

The other way a sacred tool may be acquired is by choosing an object, usually in connection with one's particular religion or spiritual path, and then going about the prescribed or self-designed steps of blessing and consecrating it prior to use. This 'transforms' the ordinary object into a magical one. Once an empowered sacred tool is in the hands of its keeper it must be treated with the highest regard. Whenever possible it should be kept in its own container so as to protect it from harm and contamination from negative influences. Often the material or animal hide within which the special object is wrapped is also from a power animal or has been especially fashioned for this particular use and purpose. As with the jewelled scabbard of Excalibur, many such containers or covers are embroidered or painted with magical symbols and/or words of power. Sometimes the owner will embellish the box, pouch or other type of covering with jewels, beads or other decorative materials so as to make it as beautiful as possible which, in and of itself, is an act of care and respect.

One's medicine tool is one's 'link' to higher levels and realms of reality. It is, often, the very 'source' of power that the shaman taps for use in propelling him into altered states of awareness so that he might be in touch with the spirits and forces that he desires. The use of such an object triggers something deep inside that grows and swells to a great intensity, and is within these levels that magic takes place when the soul takes charge and unites the mind and body in perfect harmony and balance with the forces of Nature or natural law.

Sacred objects have a life of their own. Many believe that they are actually the harbingers of indwelling, living entities and that their owners must be properly trained and consciously aware of those entities so as not to bring undue harm upon themselves or others when they recruit the object's power. Sacred objects are also our teachers. Through their proper care and use we come to a greater awareness of the higher forces in Nature and in ourselves. We learn to bridge the gap between spirit and matter. But if we mishandle or misuse a sacred tool, we open ourselves, like Arthur, to harm from the powers inherent in the object itself.

In this time when so many are seeking knowledge of the ways of shamanism and the medicine path, and as the magician archetype stirs from its slumber within the unconscious of individuals world-wide, we must come to acquaint ourselves with the sacred tools of the magical practitioner before we take them up and use them in ignorance. We must come to see and understand them as a method by which we can learn to focus our power more efficiently and effectively. Every sacred object has archetypal connections and some, such as Excalibur, are archetypes in and of themselves. They are born from the Collective Unconscious of humanity and, in that, they are universal in nature. Together, man and sword, man and pipe, man and magical wand can wield the power of harmony with all life. At the end of life's journey, as with Arthur and Excalibur, each will be returned into the mists of yesterday and tomorrow, once more blended into the fabric of Eternity.

References

1. *King Arthur and the Grail*: Richard Cavendish.
2. *The Secret Tradition in Arthurian Legend*: Gareth Knight.

6

THE HOLY GRAIL
Bridge to the Divine

The Mystery of the Holy Grail
Doth to the seeking soul avail
To give a knowledge of the Plan
The Mystery of the Christ in Man.

BEREDENE JOCELYN

There is a distinct difference between a legend and a fairy-tale, the latter being pure fantasy, the former having roots in reality. Both, however, serve the purpose of portraying and preserving particular traditions of a land and its people. Upon occasion a person or an object crosses a bridge and fits comfortably into the fabric of both realms. Such a person is King Arthur – and such an object is the Holy Grail. As the subject of a fairy-tale, the Grail is a hidden treasure that possesses magical powers that will deliver its finder from the evils of the material world; as the subject of a legend, deeply rooted in Christianity, it is the cup shared by the Christ and his disciples at the Last Supper, into which the uncle of Jesus, Joseph of Arimathea, received the blood of Jesus at the time of the crucifixion:

> *This remarkable blend of fairy-tale and legend gives the Grail stories their peculiar character, for through these stories the 'eternal' fairy-tale enters, as it were, the realm of the temporal drama of the Christian aeon and thus reflects not only fundamental human problems but also the dramatic psychic events which form the background of our Christian culture.* [1]

From the moment of its appearance on the ancient stage of oral teachings and literature alike, the Holy Grail was, and is, hailed as a marvellous object with great powers. It is not confined to either Arthurian or Christian traditions – an arcane Hellenic legend tells us of Crater, the cup within which the gods mixed the very 'stuff' of Creation, and Sufis know it as the 'Cup of Jasmid' from which the nectar of the virtues of knowledge and divine inspiration was dispensed, while others told of a particular star that fell from the crown of Lucifer, the Lord of Light, and became the vessel that held the blood of Christ. Other such glorious cups are the themes of stories in Japan, the Soviet Union and India. All possess the same or similar powers of the restoration of harmony in body, mind and soul, and bestow upon their discovers special magical knowledge and skills. Over the centuries the Grail stories have never lost their fascination and appeal. Within them is embodied a 'living myth' that still applies to contemporary men and women today. Credit for this longevity must also be given to the legendary aspects of the Grail, in that if it once existed as an actual object, then it still does, somewhere, and may be found.

In order to gain understanding of the deep significance of

the Grail it is important to investigate it from both its literal and symbolic perspectives, for each provides valuable insights for the modern spiritual seeker. I will begin with an addition to the Christian tradition that also involves Joseph of Arimathea. In *Mythology of the British Isles* by Geoffrey Ashe we learn that after the crucifixion:

> *The risen Christ appeared to him [Joseph] and taught him sacred words, through which the Grail could be the medium of a special revelation. It kept him alive without ordinary food during a long imprisonment by Jews who had been Christ's enemies. Released at last, Joseph set off with many companions on divinely-guided wanderings. They had the Grail with them, and made a table to set it on, in commemoration of the table of the Last Supper. At length these wanderings brought the Grail to Britain, to the Vales of Avalon, the future site of Glastonbury. However, it did not remain there. It passed to its hiding-place in the elusive castle, which was called Corbenic, and to a succession of keepers collaterally descended from Joseph.*

Another version of this legend tells that Joseph and his companions – who some say included the mother of Jesus and some of the disciples – built the first Christian church outside the Holy Land in Glastonbury, and the Grail was the holy relic used on its high altar. Later, to avoid it being stolen, it is said that Joseph hid the sacred chalice in the well on Chalice Hill. Although there is little or no physical evidence to support this legend, it has persisted until this day and has made the town of Glastonbury in Somerset, England, a place of pilgrimage for centuries.

The Glastonbury landscape is filled with Christian and pagan sacred sites and sanctuaries that are both natural and man-made. For generations, the town's major industry has been raw fleeces and hides. Surrounded by emerald-green hills, and home today to some 8,000 people, Glastonbury, once an island, has been known by many names. The earliest was *Ynis Witrin* or 'The Glassy Isle'. Later, because it was ideal for the cultivation of apples, it came to be called *Insula Avalonia* or 'The Isle of the Apple Trees'. It is not know for certain how it came to be known as Glastonbury, but it is widely agreed that the name was derived from the Celtic word *glas*, meaning 'green', and *ton*, meaning 'hill', the green hill.

This is made even more likely by the presence of the most dominant feature in the landscape: Glastonbury Tor. The Tor is a natural conical hill that was terraced in ancient times. It is considered by most authorities to have been the site of a Druid college and perhaps the Isle of Avalon itself. Rising 518 feet into the air, the Tor's spiralled slopes still beckon pilgrims to its summit. A bell tower, the only vestige of an old church that once stood on the top, remains as a mute grey stone sentinel over the ancient landscape, its companion buildings destroyed in an earthquake in AD 1275. Though the former island is now a grassy plain, Glastonbury was once the site of prehistoric villages of mud and wattle huts, whose inhabitants flourished and mastered sophisticated art forms that included wheel-made pottery, wheeled carts, wooden bowls skilfully decorated with artistic designs and patterns, glass beads, tin and copper ornaments, bronze figures and utensils, and even the difficult art of enamelling.

Next to the Tor lies Chalice Hill, at whose foot is located a well, fed by a spring whose origin is an underground river in the Mendip Hills to the north of the town. Known since the earliest times as the 'Chalice Well' or 'Holy Well', the flow is 25,000 gallons a day. This remains totally unaffected by climatic conditions. It is here that the Christian Grail legends begin or end, depending upon how you look at it.

One interesting aspect of the story of Joseph placing the Holy Grail in the well for safekeeping is that the water turned red, reminiscent of the blood of Christ that the cup had once held. While it is true that the well is known romantically as the 'Blood Spring' and does leave a reddish deposit over the stones where it flows, this is, in the physical sense at least, due to the high content of iron in the water. Astounding and convincing cures have been acclaimed for the waters of the Chalice Well and these may be the result of the site's special history.

Whenever I think of the Chalice Well I am reminded of one of my visits there on an early morning in the April of 1990. I strolled slowly through the lovely gardens and listened to the songs of the birds mingling joyfully with the soft fragrance of the flowers, each giving the garden an air of gentle unworldliness that made any idea of conflict anywhere on Earth completely foreign to my consciousness. The words of William Blake came flowing through my mind like a melodious hymn:

> And did those feet in ancient times
> Walk upon England's mountains green?
> And was the Holy Lamb of God
> On England's pleasant pastures seen?

Some say that Jesus himself came to Glastonbury long ago. My thoughts drifted to those 'ancient times' when, perhaps, the Master himself had walked in the very place where I was . . . so long ago. I felt close to the Master Jesus that morning, closer than I had felt in a long time. My heart sensed his gentleness – what a gentle, kind man he must have been. I went up an easy incline and caught a glimpse of the water of the Chalice Well pouring forth from a lion's head carved from stone, adding an even deeper sense of peace to my already tranquil state. I sat on a bench nearby the sacred well, soaking in the healing energy of that morning, the garden, the whole place. Never before had I experienced such a sense of inner quiet and peace, as if I were all soul, not human, just soul – protected, loved, grateful for my life. Could the Grail itself have once been here? Could it still be here?

If the Chalice Well were indeed a hiding place for the Holy Grail (Chalice = Grail?), it was only a temporary one. Legend has it that the holy cup was kept at Glastonbury, either hidden safely away in the well or kept as the central holy relic on the high altar at Glastonbury Abbey until the time of the Crusades, when it was entrusted to the Crusaders only to be lost in a battle at Antioch. It is interesting to note that in 1910 a cup was retrieved at an archaeological dig in Antioch by Arab excavators. That chalice was said to be of plain design and made of silver. It was sent to the United States at the outbreak of the First World War and some scholars think it possible that it may be the cup of the Last Supper.

Aside from the acceptance of the Grail legend by early Christians world-wide and its connections with Glastonbury, it is the Grail's link with the Arthurian legends that interests me the most. If we approach the Holy Grail from the perspective of its role within the Arthurian saga, it becomes even clearer that King Arthur's court, its characters and their adventures form the basis for the teachings of an ancient Mystery School. Follow this thought: the appearance of the Grail in the Arthurian myths comes after its disappearance from the *physical* world. In various traditions, Truth, embodied in this instance in the Holy Grail, disappears from time to time from the physical world and the wisdoms go out of mankind's reach. Perhaps such times are when the world is saturated with evil to the point that humanity turns away from knowing and living the Truth, or when mankind has not evolved enough to take on the responsibilities necessary to maintain balance and harmony. The reappearance of the Truth gives fallen humanity a way to come, once more, to the Great Throne of the Ancients, to recover lost knowledge. In these current troubled times in our modern world this could be happening again. The Truth, the Holy Grail, is returning once more to guide humanity towards the Light of awareness.

When the Grail reappeared in the Arthurian legends, as best I can determine, it came through the vision of a holy nun who was the sister of Perceval, one of the knights of the Round Table. While she prayed and fasted to dispel the evils of man and the world, the Grail manifested before her eyes, rose-red in colour with markings on it. It seemed alive and was accompanied by the celestial sounds of angelic music. The appearance of the Grail ushered in a year of miracles during which the famed Galahad came to Arthur's court and was knighted by the king. It was during the knighting ceremony that the thinly veiled Grail appeared, seen clearly only by Galahad himself. Inspired by the vision, Gawain vowed to go in search of the Grail for 12 months and a day and not to return until he had seen it unveiled in all its splendour. Other knights followed Gawain's initiative and what followed is one of the greatest legends of gallantry and personal quest, peppered with the most ardent enthusiasm and idealism, that literature has ever recorded.

It is within the various segments of the knights' search that we find the true meaning and value of the Grail itself and learn of its implications for the spiritual seeker today. In order to explore this, it is important that we know of the whereabouts of the sacred cup during its time of 'withdrawal' from the physical world, prior to its appearance at Arthur's court. I found the best retelling of the basic story in the introduction to *The Grail Legends* by Emma Jung and Marie von Franz:

> *A mysterious, life-preserving and sustenance-dispensing object or vessel is guarded by a King in a castle that is difficult to find. The King is either lame or sick and the surrounding country is devastated. The King can only be restored to health if a knight of conspicuous excellence finds the castle and at the first sight of what he sees there asks a certain question. Should he neglect to put this question, then everything will remain as before, the castle will vanish and the knight will have to set out once more upon the search. Should he finally succeed, after much wandering and many adventures, in finding the Grail Castle again, and should he then ask 'the' question, the King will be restored to health, the land will begin to grow green, and the hero will become the guardian of the Grail from that time on.*

Sometimes the monarch of the legend is referred to as the Fisher King for, after having been wounded in battle by a javelin, he can neither walk nor ride, and fishing is his only pastime. It is in this nickname that we catch the first subtle glimpse of the archetypal nature of the king himself. It is interesting to note that the *fish* often appears in Christian legends as the food that satisfied the hunger of those present – in the feeding of the five thousand and at the Grail table of Joseph of Arimathea, for example. Furthermore, in several religions, the fish is regarded as a symbol of the 'saviour'. Jung and von Franz also point out another, deeper perspective of the fish:

> *The fish, living in the darkness of deep water, is often illustrative of a content of the* unconscious *[roman mine] that lingers below the threshold of consciousness and in which instinctual and*

spiritual aspects are still merged in an undifferentiated state.
Therefore, the fish is the inspirer, a bringer of wisdom and, at the
same time, a helpful animal – at once insight and redemptive,
instinctive impulse. [2]

Thus, the Fisher King becomes the seeker of inner knowledge and, as monarch, the representative of the people and the centre of the kingdom. This image may easily be translated into the Self who incarnates and becomes involved in the perils of life and who, ultimately, attains salvation. Also, among primitive peoples, the king represents the life of the people and it is upon him that they depend for sustenance and security. In past times, whenever the king fell ill and was unable to fulfil his role for society he was often killed so that a healthy successor might reign. But we do not see the death of the Fisher King, and the reason for this may lie in Jung's and von Franz's idea that this particular image may represent a 'stricken society'. It would follow that the stricken king fishing portrays humanity searching for spiritual guidance and redemption to cure its ills, not unlike society today. And salvation is guaranteed, individually and collectively, by the very existence of the Grail, guarded by the Self/soul in the hidden castle/human unconscious. Again, where is the Grail hidden? In a castle described as 'difficult to find'. There can be little doubt that the Grail Castle must be taken to exist in the Otherworld which, according to traditional Celtic lore, was held to be an island or under the water. This links the castle with water, which has long been associated with the astral world and the human subconscious, indicating that we must pursue the Grail in areas *within* ourselves that lie below the surface of ordinary waking consciousness and in places, so to speak, that exist only within the imagination, the tool of psychic insight.

Another link between the Grail and water is made by two aquatic birds, the pelican and the swan, which have both long been symbols of the Holy Cup. The swan is the symbol of the Grail Knight who is initiated into the Mysteries of the Christ, whereas the pelican is the symbol of the Christ Truth or knowledge of the Divine Mystery. It is interesting to point out that the swan also corresponds to the name given to the constellation Cygnus, which can be seen in the northern skies and is sometimes referred to as the 'Northern Cross', due, no doubt, to its resemblance to the cross of the crucifixion. I think that this is an indication that the Great Mysteries were embodied in the stars, and perhaps originated there, an idea that I shall explore later.

The Grail Quest was filled with demons, dragons and peril of all kinds and took the knights into worlds terrible and sublime. Such is the nature of the landscape of the inner human consciousness. The path that we follow in search of meaningful existence and personal validity, arcane wisdom and true spiritual awareness is one that is filled with the obstacles of doubt, greed, sorrow, pain, abuse and misuse of power, and falsehoods that confront us. Each of us has to struggle to overcome these obstructions so we can reach out and partake of the contents of the Grail, our divine inheritance of health, sustenance and immortality.

When coming into the presence of the Holy Grail, the knights were told to ask a crucial question: 'What is the Grail?' or 'To whom shall this cup be given?' Asking the question would heal the Fisher King and break the evil spell over the castle. This is considered by some scholars to have to do with the line of succession to the throne. However, I think there are various meanings involved with the 'question' – or perhaps one answer that has many levels within it.

On one level the Grail is the *soul* of man and the human

search for the soul is life's greatest quest and one that we all have in common. But the soul may only be discovered by those who have overcome the obstacles and removed the veils, if you will, that stand in the way of the purity and innocence of the soul and the dimension within which it resides. On another level, the Grail is the vessel that contains all esoteric wisdom, the Great Mystery. Furthermore, it is the giver of redemption and absolute prosperity. And finally, as pointed out so aptly by Gareth Knight, it is:

> . . . that which is left out of the Christian Holy Trinity of Father, Son and Holy Spirit. It is the divine feminine in mankind and in Nature. It is Father-Mother, the polarized and shared forces in Creation and Creator, thus pulling the female principle out of the darkness and evil domain of Eve, the temptress, and into quality and harmony with the male force in all things.[3]

This idea is reinforced in some versions of the Grail legends where the Grail is identified as a holy vessel of the Divine that is carried in procession by a woman who represents a fertility goddess. This is an obvious reference to the Cup as a symbol of woman who is the channel through which all life enters into the physical world. This relationship to the feminine firmly establishes the Grail as a symbol of the womb of life and fertility which must be raised up from degradation if we are to truly understand the complete esoteric picture and know the full impact of the duality of Nature. Recognition of both these universal principles, their functions and manifestations in all things, is crucial in the evolution of human consciousness, as is coming to live in harmony with them. This is the very key to initiation.

On the purely human level, the Grail is related to the human heart – our spiritual receptacle, if you will. Perhaps, ultimately, it is the heart, not the mind, that must transform what is gained through experience and what is learned by the intellect into wisdom. Perhaps the mind allows us to see the *outside* of the Grail, that is, maybe we can find the Grail by walking the path of knowledge and experience and by working with ceremony to help accomplish the attainment of the so-called 'Lesser Mysteries' of classical antiquity. But on the other hand, we need an open heart to help us see the *inside* of the Grail, and in doing so, access the 'Greater Mysteries' that are achieved by a union with the Divine.

Among the Knights of the Round Table most often associated with the Holy Grail it is Perceval and Galahad who bear the closest investigation. These personalities are intertwined, in that they were both knights, both are often referred to as the 'perfect knight', and each, at one time or another, was considered to be the hero of the Grail Quest. That these figures are archetypal in nature cannot be denied.

Perceval, who first appears to us through the unfinished writings of Chrétien de Troyes in the twelfth century, is the overprotected child, kept ignorant of chivalry by his mother, who blamed it for her husband's death. But upon learning of the existence of knights, the lad disregards his mother's grief and fears, and runs away to Arthur's court where he receives basic training to be a knight. Upon hearing of the Grail, Perceval impulsively sets off on an adventurous and successful search for the Grail Castle. Once inside the castle, he sees the Grail Procession but, having been told not to talk unless necessary, does not ask the question. Later he learns that the question would have cured the stricken king.

It is important to remember that Perceval had only the most basic knightly training, which surely contributes to his portrayal as a knight who is gallant and brave, but lacking in terms of responsibility and understanding. Obviously Perceval did not know the difference between idle chatter and necessary talk, for example. If Jung's and von Franz's idea is correct and the Fisher King is indeed symbolic of a 'stricken society', then Perceval's shortcoming robs him, as a knight, of the opportunity to help cure the ills of society and help put humanity back on the course of greater harmony with the universe.

Although the unfortunate knight sets out to right his sin of omission, the unfinished state de Troyes' poem leaves his quest eternally incomplete. We learn, however, from the various descriptions of the Perceval character some of the requirements of the Grail Quest. To begin with, we have to be absolutely prepared for the tasks we set out to accomplish. Perceval did not recognize, perhaps, the depths or limits of his own power and capability, which would have surely been the origin of his failure. Clearly, he was intrigued by the quest itself more than by its actual attainment and the responsibilities that came along with it. He jumped into the quest on impulse; he did not plan or organize his thoughts and actions. How often we do this ourselves. We jump into things without considering the consequences or without a strategy for the attainment of our goal. In Perceval I am reminded of an old cliché: 'Be careful what you ask for, you might get it'! Perceval did get his wish. He saw the Grail Procession – that is, he reached the gate, so to speak. He had just enough courage for that, just enough knowledge, just enough initiatory training to accomplish these feats where others had failed. Still it wasn't enough. When it came to the moment of making the grade on the practical level, he failed. He knew just enough to *feel* the power but not enough to *handle* it. Such a degree of knowledge can be more dangerous than beneficial. Knowledge alone is not enough. We have to be able to *apply* that knowledge to daily life under various and changing conditions. Only then does it become true wisdom.

Galahad, on the other hand, holds the title of the perfect Grail Knight. Son of Sir Lancelot and Elaine, he was conceived, as already related, when Lancelot was under the influence of a potion that caused him to think that he was with Guinevere. The youngest knight ever, Galahad arrived at Arthur's court in the latter years of its existence; his arrival, like that of Arthur, already foreseen, following various signs and unusual events. A stone of red marble came down the river near Camelot and lodged itself near the shore. In the marble was a sword which bore an inscription stating that it could only be removed by the 'best knight in the world'. Lancelot denied that this could refer to him, for he was unworthy, and although Perceval and Gawain tried, they both failed. Later, while Arthur and his knights were seated around the Round Table, the doors of the hall flew open and revealed an old man dressed in white robes and a youth, Galahad, who was clad in red garments and who did not wear the armour of a knight. There was an empty scabbard by his side, which we later learn was made for him by Perceval's sister. The belt for the scabbard was made from her hair – hair is often symbolic of vitality as it is that closest to the mind. Galahad was led to the Round Table's empty seat, the Siège Perilous, after the old man had dressed him in a crimson robe decorated with ermine. The Siège Perilous was inscribed with letters that no one had been able to decipher, but as the lad approached it, its words became clear for all to read: 'This is the seat of Sir Galahad, the Good Knight.' Galahad passed the test of the Perilous Seat and the sword in the stone, and was thus recognized as the one who would be the future hero of the Grail Quest.

An intriguing detail regarding Galahad is that he remained a virgin throughout his life. This is obviously an indication of his physical and literal as well as his symbolic purity, and has also been given as having compensated for the impure circumstances surrounding his conception. The young knight was proclaimed as physically beautiful, morally perfect and the possessor of physical prowess unmatched by any other knight. He had the required virtues to look upon the Grail and partake of its rewards. It was Galahad who healed the Fisher King, only to die from the ecstasy of seeing, firsthand, the marvels and glory of the Grail itself. I believe that this signifies the shedding of the body physical and the freeing of the soul into the higher realms of existence. No man has looked upon the face of God and lived.

During his quest for the Holy Grail, Galahad had three major encounters, each typifying a human challenge to be met and overcome. I believe that it is within these encounters that we find the elements that actually comprise the path of discipleship every one of us will walk during earthly existence. The encounters are a 'formula' and deserve exploration, albeit basic and brief.

The first encounter I shall refer to as the 'Challenge in the Valley of Camelot'. It is here that Galahad meets the 'Loathly Damsel' and her two companions. These three are symbolic of the three lower aspects of human consciousness, namely the ego or personality, the etheric self and the astral self, which are, collectively, regarded as the desire body or the emotional/base self. There is no greater power that man must gain control over than that of his inner feelings and desires. Desires are born from the power of emotions and what we feel is the driving force behind who and what we are and what we will become. The Loathly Damsel, an ugly maiden once very beautiful, verbally lashes out at the young knight, blaming him for the terrible condition in which she finds herself. Rather than denying any blame for her situation, as most would do, Galahad *admits* responsibility!

A powerful wisdom may be gleaned from this admission when we stop to consider how each of us is responsible for the loathsome images, in the form of negative feelings, that we allow entrance into our mind and consciousness and, in turn, into our bodies and soul. Some are created by our own imagination and have their roots in our negative emotions, while others are created by others but erroneously accepted as our own. We must remember that we have control over what we think and feel. We are the creators of our own condition. If that condition is negative, it affects the whole of our lives. By the willing acceptance of blame for the ugliness of the Loathly Damsel, Galahad sets himself aside from the ordinary human, and after attaining the Grail he is able to transform her back into her beautiful self. The damsel's transformation is indicative of what is possible when the awakening of the Divine occurs within us, while Galahad's actions show what can come from the recognition of our role, as individuals, in the whole human condition. All too often we prefer to stand and defend ourselves, denying responsibility for any part in the ugliness we see around us. 'What can *I* do?' is the usual response. But we learn from Galahad that we can do a great deal – by the realization of our own role in creating ugliness we can transform it into beauty. This enables us to manifest beauty and wisdom and to dispel ignorance and darkness once and for all from ourselves and our lives. Ultimately, this can lead to a world cleansing.

The second challenge I shall call the 'Challenge of the Seven Evil Brothers'. In this episode, Galahad must meet and engage in mortal combat with seven evil brothers, each of whom wears a dark grey suit of armour and stands guard over a castle that imprisons seven lovely and pure maidens. One by one the brothers are conquered. These seven evil brothers represent the seven deadly sins of mankind: anger, laziness, greed, pride, gluttony, envy and lust. In overcoming these obstacles inherent in human nature, Galahad gained a greater purity which permitted him to progress further down the path of discipleship to confront even greater challenges.

Note that the colour of dark grey is mentioned in the description of the armour worn by the evil brothers. Grey, when seen in the human aura, denotes fear, which some would say is the source of all human failing. Galahad overcame fear in defeating the brothers, and fear may very well be the final obstacle that keeps us completely human.

The seven pure maidens of this challenge are symbols of the chakras found in the human etheric body. These are vortices where energy is received and emitted by an incarnate human being. Primarily an aspect of Eastern metaphysics, knowledge of the workings of the chakras forms an integral part of the process of discipleship. Awareness begins in the lower chakras and, as one grows closer to the Light, the higher ones are opened and activated, namely the heart, throat, third eye and crown, known as the seat of the soul. The maidens' castles are one's own inner self in which exists the various dimensions of human consciousness and reality inherent within each of us. These are levels or realms through which one must travel so that, eventually, enlightenment is attained.

At the defeat of the seven evil brothers, an old man appears to Galahad and presents him with the key to all the castles of the maidens. It is clear that the old man represents wisdom and the key is the virtue Galahad has gained in his conquests: self-control. None of us may come to know true self-control until the obstacles of the deadly sins are met and overcome. Such is the purpose of living. Along the way, in some lifetime, however, we too will receive the 'key'. Then and only then will we be ready and qualified to go further along the path.

The third and final challenge of Galahad I shall call the 'Carbonek Experience'. At Carbonek, said by some to be the Grail Castle, Galahad finds Sir Perceval and Sir Bors, both of whom were on the Grail Quest, along with nine other knights: three from Gaul, three from Denmark and three from Ireland. Perceval and Bors have failed in their attempts to attain the Grail, but may now witness the success of Galahad. Perhaps the symbology of the nine knights is an indication of the lands within which is wisdom was entrusted and, therefore, significant of political as well as spiritual alliance. I cannot be sure.

At the time of this challenge, the correct question is asked by Galahad, and as a result, the Fisher King is healed of his infirmaries and the Grail Castle freed from its spell. When the king has departed, Galahad sees a vision of four angels descending from Heaven carrying a chair upon which is seated his ancestor, Joseph of Arimathea. The angels place the chair bearing Joseph in front of a silver table upon which stands the Holy Grail. Next, the door opens and four more angels come in, two carrying candles, one a towel and the other a bleeding lance or spear. The blood drips into a bowl the angel carries in the other hand. The angels place all of the sacred objects on the table with the Grail and Joseph serves Mass. As this is being done, Galahad sees the vision of a child in the bread as it is being placed in the Cup. Each of the knights is given Communion and the kiss of peace. Joseph disappears and the Christ appears from the Cup and administers its contents to the knights. The Christ then announces that the Sacred Cup must now be hidden from mankind due to the rampant evil in the land. He requests that Galahad take the Grail to Sarras, the spiritual place, once more. After doing this, Galahad is stricken with ecstasy and ascends to Heaven.

The appearance of Joseph of Arimathea here is indicative of the lineage of the wisdom teachings and the fact that Christianity has possession of them within its pure doctrine. The angels may indeed be symbolic not only of those who have possession of the Grail and guard it, but also perhaps of the 'originators' of the wisdoms who, in turn, passed them to mankind. Some say that this is the meaning behind the so-called 'Fall' in the Bible. The lance is the one that wounded the crucified Christ and the towel that which wrapped the newborn messiah and also received his body at his interment in the tomb. The candles are symbols of the Light itself as well as the tools that shed light upon the path of the aspirant's life. In this way, they are reminiscent of The Hermit in the Tarot, for The Hermit, symbolic of the adept of the hidden knowledge, holds a light in his hand and holds it up high so that its rays might illumine the way. All of these, together, are the births and deaths and pains and sufferings that we all encounter along the road of physical life. And from the sacred cup we receive access to and communion with the Mysteries, which leads to heavenly bliss.

Only the pure can go to Sarras, the spiritual place. It is a place where the initiates live, comparable to Shambala in the Eastern teachings. This is clearly the final stage of the initiation process. The quest is complete. The Perfect Knight has looked into the face of the Christ, the King of the Mysteries. As with the other challenges, there is much to be learned from this last vision and experience of Galahad, and I must add a thought regarding the appearance of the angels. Seen as 'agents' of Divinity, angels work with humanity in a karmic bond of the need and desire to be of benefit to humanity and, in that way, the Shining Ones fulfil their own karmic responsibilities to Creation and the

Creator. I find it most exciting that in our present day there is a resurgence of mass interest in angels and their work. Numerous books have begun to appear, some reprinted from earlier, much older manuscripts, and others based on new, contemporary experiences and visions. If the Light is entrusted to angels, then there can be little doubt that they are seeking to make themselves known once again to our troubled world.

I have already mentioned some startling similarities between Galahad and King Arthur: the birth of both was predicted, both were conceived with the aid of magic, both pulled a sword from a stone as an act that revealed their true identity, and neither died – Arthur is taken to Avalon and Galahad ascends to Heaven. I think that this indicates a karmic bond between these two souls. But there is more to it than that. Where Arthur failed, Galahad succeeded. In spite of his good deeds, Arthur does not emerge as the one who achieved Enlightenment. If he had done so, this would have meant the end of the kingdom, the Round Table, everything. But in Galahad we have the aspirant fulfilling the quest. This lets us know that we can reach our goals. The quest can be completed by humans. The adventures of the knights and King Arthur show us what we do wrong that trips us up. But where Arthur failed, Galahad shows us that we can succeed; we can overcome all dangers and obstacles. The wisdoms are safe and will descend when necessary and when humanity is open to receive them.

From a different viewpoint, Arthur is the 'caretaker' of mankind and the land. Galahad is related to the Christ. Without Arthur there would have been no court, no knights, no Round Table, no Grail Quest for Galahad to fulfil. And without Galahad there would have been no one in the Arthurian epic pure enough to reach the highest level of initiation possible by way of the western occult tradition so beautifully concealed in these characters and events.

Finally, concerning the failure of all the knights except Galahad in the Grail Quest, an interesting point is made by Gareth Knight when, commenting specifically upon Lancelot, he states: 'Human devotion is not necessarily a fault in itself. It is simply inappropriate in the context of one who desires to make the unreserved dedication to the service of higher forces and is impelled thereby to fall away.' Knight further shows us that few of the knights were candidates for the level of initiation symbolized by the Grail Quest and that their experiences, therefore, were uneventful and hold no special meaning for us. I agree, other than commenting that we stand to gain from learning from the knights' individual personality traits, which we all possess and which all manifest in some way at one time or another in our lives. Knight compares this with the general consciousness of the masses who, when faced with comprehension of the Higher Mysteries or the true meaning of life's events 'become impatient of any advice on the matter and soon find good reason to give up the apparently useless and fruitless Quest'. I think that it is important to recognize that when we are following a chosen spiritual path we must at some point be able to express ourselves aptly and fully as human beings, but not allow our 'humanness' to sway us from our chosen course and spiritual vision.

You may be interested to note that during ancient Atlantean times, in the city squares, there were great fountains shaped like the Holy Cup, with water overflowing their rim. [This suggests that the Grail was a symbol that was sacred long before King Arthur's time or Christianity or any other religion or culture.] Daily, seven times, people would come and drink from the fountain as an act and symbol of replenishment and nourishment . . . a quenching of their spiritual thirst.

CHANNELLED BY ALBION

References

1. *The Grail Legend*: Emma Jung and Marie Louise von Franz.
2. Ibid.
3. *The Secret Tradition in Arthurian Legend*: Gareth Knight.

THE GODDESS CONNECTION

Discovering the Woman Within

She who is first of them is more skilled in the healing art, and excels her sisters in the beauty of her person. Morgan is her name, and she has learned what useful properties all the herbs contain, so that she can cure sick bodies. She also knows an art by which to change her shape, and to cleave the air on new wings like Daedalus.
GEOFFREY OF MONMOUTH, *VITA MERLINI*

Women played an integral role in the life of King Arthur. His beautiful mother, Igraine, his enchanting half-sister, Morgan, his tempestuous and lovely wife, Guinevere, all in their own way brought light or darkness into the king's life as the incredible drama of their lives unfolded. As I continue my study in the Matter of Britain it becomes more apparent to me that the legends have indeed changed with the telling. Times change, and with the firm establishment of Christianity in Great Britain the stories were coloured by its values and belief system, which often clashed with the pagan values that had reigned for so long. The Arthurian legends became intriguing 'mixtures' of the two, and for this reason the major feminine characters have two dimensions or roles. One is a purely human identity; the other a symbolic one, as each major female character is the human embodiment of a goddess of the old Celtic tradition. Each is an archetype revealing specific 'patterns' of human behaviour. In addition, as participants in the lives of Arthur, Lancelot and Merlin, like them, they represent aspects of an ancient esoteric tradition. These are female characters who initiate physical, emotional, mental and spiritual tests of will and strength to those around them.

Myths have many layers of reality and meaning. To get the most from them we must be aware of the many levels of life and of the individual human being. This is how we come to realize that even if the characters in the Arthurian myths *were* truly historical figures, the reason they are known all over the world and have survived for hundreds of years is because they strike a stirring note within the human psyche. In *Women in Celtic Mythology*, Moyra Caldicott echoes this:

> *We understand these stories, although technologically and in many other superficial ways our societies are very different, because they are about human beings, who, like us, are on a journey learning painfully, step by step, to fulfil our considerable potential – faced them, as now, with the same essential problems, sorrows and delights, beset from within and without by the same dark and violent shadows.*

In light of the male and female roles that are being played

out in our modern society, however, it may be difficult to understand the men and women of fifth-century Britain. What we may consider normal and acceptable behaviour would not have been tolerated then. Our present-day attitudes regarding adultery, male chauvinism, commitment and a woman's 'place' in personal relationships and in society differ immensely from those of that time. We also have to keep in mind the code of chivalry and its effect upon human relationships and values. In short, we must learn to put ourselves in the shoes of those who lived long ago, in a unique and exciting era, far removed, for better or worse, from the twentieth century. Also, we must remember that in discussing the women of the Arthurian legends, we are considering ladies of privilege and royalty and this, in and of itself, often dictated not only the public roles they would play, but also their degree of freedom. Their status also flavoured their emotional responses to their situation.

In Arthur's time women held the strings that led to the biological, political and spiritual past and they also guaranteed and coloured the future. They nursed the sick and raised the children. If a woman was highly born she was often married off for the sake of good political alliance. For such women, being able to provide an heir for the preservation of the lineage was of paramount importance. Some of them, however, lived outside domestic life, dwelling within both the natural and supernatural worlds, symbolically uniting matter and spirit into a bond of power and intrigue.

Unravelling the characters of Igraine, Morgan and Guinevere and their contribution to the deeper meanings of the myths that envelop their lives is but another leg of our journey of self-discovery. These women are within each of us, no matter what our gender. Carl Jung said that there is a man in every woman and a woman in every man!

Realization of this fundamental psychological truth can have very practical applications in our individual lives. Discovering our own indwelling feminine power and learning how it operates and how it manifests itself and affects our behaviour can go far in helping us understand ourselves. By exploring Igraine, Morgan and Guinevere, I will seek to present both their human and archetypal qualities. They are mother, priestess, sorceress, seductress, wife, adulteress and lover.

The first woman who appears prominently in the Arthurian legends is the mother of the future king. Igraine (Ygerna) was, as the Duchess of Cornwall and wife of Duke Gorlois, the First Lady of the minor royalty of that seaside kingdom in south-western England. According to modern versions of the legends,[1] she had come into this Christian household from a pagan background for she was sister to the priestess, Vivianne, who once held the position of Lady of the Lake in Avalon. Even though Igraine had converted to Christianity, in her heart she still held to the Old Religion. Ironically, it was this belief that had sealed her fate. In many modern retellings, it was through a 'vision' of Vivianne's that Igraine came to marry Gorlois, pushed into it by her sister for the purpose of bringing about a political alliance that would help to ensure the future of the country.

Igraine's home was the hauntingly beautiful castle of Tintagel, believed by some to have been built by the Ancient Ones from the lost land of Lyonnesse, allegedly a part of the fabled Atlantis before it sank off the Cornish coast. The castle, now in ruins, once perched precariously at the end of a long causeway which stretches out into the sparkling blue Atlantic.

Cornwall's strategic location made it valuable military real estate. When Arthur became king, many of his knights came from the West Country and formed what came to be known as the 'Cornish connection'. Igraine was treated as an equal to her husband except in military matters, and as a result of the comfortable conditions of her life she was content if not entirely happy. However, amidst her protected world there were personal matters of a highly sensitive and emotional nature that the duchess had to deal with, for although Duke Gorlois was a generous husband, he wanted something in return: he wanted a son.

Though versions of the lineages differ, Igraine is usually credited with three daughters from a previous marriage and one daughter, Morgan, by Gorlois. But Romans reckoned their lineage through the father rather than through the mother and Gorlois was of Roman descent. No doubt there were bastard sons, for the Duke was a warrior who spent much time away from home and such men did not think twice about fathering children out of wedlock. But such children did not count. Only a son by his wife could be Gorlois' legal and rightful heir. Alas, as fate would have it, he was never to have a son by Igraine. Their world was to be changed forever by the desires of Uther Pendragon, the reigning High King of Britain. The reader will recall that knowing that Igraine would never commit an act of adultery, Merlin devised a magical plot whereby Uther could come to her in the guise of her husband. The same night that Arthur was conceived, Gorlois, who was away in battle, was killed. Soon afterwards Uther was wedded to Igraine.

The biological role of Igraine as Arthur's mother is clear enough. But as we begin to unravel her symbolic qualities we discover some interesting points. In the compelling work of Gareth Knight Igraine is described in a most unique way as 'an *Atlantean* [italics mine] princess brought over from the old civilization to mate with one of the ruling line of the new civilization. Arthur therefore has within him the blood of the ancient British kings and also the sacred blood of the Atlantean priest-kings.'[2] Assuming for the moment that Knight is correct, this certainly adds an intriguing and deeply esoteric dimension to Igraine and to the reason why she was 'chosen' to be the mother of Arthur. Perhaps some background for Knight's conclusions will be helpful here.

In the nineteenth century the Russian-born occultist H.P. Blavatsky presented the concept of what she called the 'root races' of humanity. The root races, which have their origin in Esoteric Buddhism, are seven in number. The first four have come into and passed out of existence, one absorbing the other, so to speak, and resulting in the continual *refinement* of the human species, both in physical form and in consciousness. To my understanding it is the root race to which Knight makes reference, the race that marked the beginning of the Aryans who are commonly known as Atlanteans. The legacy of the Atlantean era involves the development of the intellect and speech. The Atlanteans also had an effect on human life and consciousness. Knight presents an interesting scenario of the collective Atlantean consciousness. In a description that I find to be unique and extremely revealing, he compares the general Atlantean population to children who had a closer relationship with 'nature, with the unconscious, [and] with the Great Mother, than our own highly individualised souls of today'. Knight postulates the existence of a 'group soul', which he states was deliberately constructed through magical means by the Atlantean priesthood, who could easily mould the 'comparatively undeveloped early races'. It was this 'group soul' of the ancient past that, when mingled with the concrete intellectual minds and aestheticism of later races, produced, through time, the various national/cultural group souls that exist today. In this way, the 'seeds' of one civilization were sown into another. Knight's information can, I think, lead to a clear understanding of the evolution of the consciousness of humanity.

On the spiritual level, the Atlantean priesthood gave life to a tradition that cradled an esoteric formula for understanding the natural world, including the heavens and celestial phenomena, the secret life of plants, animals and minerals, and, according to Blavatsky, an explanation of 'the change which takes place imperceptibly in everything in this Universe from the globe down to the atom – without cessation'. If Igraine were indeed a direct 'link' to this esoteric tradition, then its very survival would have been assured by its firm indoctrination into the 'new' civilization in Britain. This also gives the Matter of Britain the 'seeds' necessary to ensure it becomes the foundation of the next or fifth root race, constituting a 'turning point' in the overall cycle of human development. Through the choice of Igraine as mother to the future king of Britain, her life energy melded the old and new lineages together. This, in turn, was passed on to Arthur. Based on Knight's commentary, we see that the manifestation of this 'seed' carried with it a sort of 'psychic sight' that later enabled Arthur, as Igraine's offspring, to communicate with both 'inner and outer' worlds and forces.

For the most part, the last we see of Igraine is when Arthur is taken from her and turned over to Merlin. During his childhood, Arthur was never influenced by his natural mother and, by all accounts, he was kept in the dark about his real parentage.

Igraine is both mother to Arthur and his half-sister, Morgan, later known as Morgan le Fay, Queen of the Fairies and heiress to the throne of Avalon. In modern myth, she is also sister to Vivianne, the Lady of the Lake, High Priestess of the Isle. Because Avalon plays such an integral role in the

Arthurian saga and is a place that figures so prominently in Arthur's life and in the lives of the women around him, it bears investigation here.

Geoffrey of Monmouth tells of Avalon being an 'otherworldly' island of Celtic mythology. Its name is the Celtic for 'the apple place'. It is depicted as a wonderful land where grain and vines grow unattended and whose inhabitants enjoy extreme longevity. Also Avalon is the home of a holy order of priestesses whose leader is the Lady of the Lake. The Order is adept at treating and healing the sick, controlling the weather, foretelling the future and interpreting signs and omens, as well as being the keepers of herbal, celestial and magical knowledge. Time and again we see Avalon appearing and playing a profound role in Arthur's life.

One of the first of these is in Merlin's influence in the rearing of the future king, as the magician may well have had connections with the Holy Isle. Another is when Arthur receives the magical sword, Excalibur, from the lake – a metaphor for Avalon. According to some legends, the sword was actually forged for him by the Lady of the Lake herself. Also, at the end of Arthur's life, he was taken to Avalon and put into the care of Morgan le Fay, who at that time was the High Priestess of the sacred island.

Somewhere in the unfolding of time Avalon came to be associated with Glastonbury. As already mentioned, an early name of Glastonbury was *Ynis Witrin* or 'The Glassy Isle'. An island of glass was a common form and description of the 'Otherworld' of the Celts.

The enchanted island was surrounded by concealing mists. It could only be seen by those with 'the sight' and only be reached by those who knew the way. There are many such places in the Arthurian legends – enchanted castles, countries and islands that are distinct from the everyday physical world. In addition to Avalon, these include the land of Gorre, the Grail Castle, the Castle of the Maidens, the Fair Unknown, the Castle Perilous encountered by the knight Gareth, and the home of Lancelot, Joyous Gard. These all exist on the astral plane, mysteriously real, passing in and out of physical manifestation throughout the legends.

The forest is also often an 'otherworldly' place. According to Richard Cavendish, 'The forest is an Otherworld, a realm which man has not tamed.'[3] Such etheric places may be places of evil but, as a rule, they possess both positive and negative aspects. Cavendish describes the forest as metaphorically concealing 'beings and secrets older, wiser, and infinitely more powerful than man'. 'The uncanny forest represents the dark depths of the mind, the tangled growths of the unconscious, "old" and "wild" in the sense of being primitive, instinctive, and unmastered by reason.'[4] We recall that Perceval ran away from the forest to become a knight and, in doing so, came out of the darkness into the light, out of ignorance into knowledge, and out of the wilds into civilization.

However, the most interesting view of both the forest and places like Avalon is when they are recognized as places where the power of 'the feminine' is at work. This power is personified by priestesses, maidens, damsels of questionable character, seductresses and fairy queens or fays who bring their power to bear, constructively or destructively, upon men. Avalon is the home of the faery women who represent Atlantean 'female chiefs and high priestesses' in the Arthurian tales. 'Today their forces are preserved in female esoteric groups and must be applied to modern times.'[5]

A point must be made here regarding the application of the old wisdoms and ways to modern times. Today, obviously, we live in a different world to that of our ancestors. We are faced with different problems. Therefore the old teachings must be adapted to suit our modern lifestyle, to meet our current needs and to cure our present ills. If not, they simply will not work for us or, worse, they will backfire, becoming a destructive force in our lives and society.

Another important side note is necessary here to remind the reader that in pagan times, realms and religion, the female force was the principal force in the universe, though it has since been displaced by Judaeo-Christianity. The concept of 'the feminine' was known and understood by religions far older than Christianity and all ancient goddesses had a three-fold nature which I shall discuss further with regard to Morgan le Fay.

In any event, once the Goddess was replaced by the male God, society became patriarchal and the status of women was reduced immensely. A woman became the harbinger of an inherent 'evil' which, through seduction of various forms, could usurp a male's masculinity, lead him into danger or make him her 'slave'. We are all familiar with the relation of Eve to the concept of 'original sin', and various prominent male Arthurian characters were negatively influenced by women. Sometimes this was because the women were pagan, and other times it was simply because they were women. This is the case with Guinevere and the pain she brought to both Arthur and Lancelot. Women could not be trusted, on the one hand, while on the other hand, they were the object of every male emotion from simple curiosity to idealistic adoration! To please his lady was the aim and vow of every knight. So what follows is that even though *all* women were suspect to a degree, the truly *evil* feminine aspects were attributed to the priestess-sorceresses who were the embodiment of the Great Mother.

All of this not only reduced women's social and religious status but also implanted an instinctual distrust and fear of women in general which is still evident, to some degree, within our modern society. The fall of the Great Mother Goddess, due to the rise of Christianity as the dominant religion, also reduced the knowledge and practice of the Old Tradition to mere sorcery. Knowledge of the old ways was, like women, considered evil and feared by the masses. In the figures of Arthur and Lancelot, however, we see individuals who were taught the arcane knowledge as a part of their upbringing, enabling them to bridge the gap between the old and new views of women. This is why they could deal with the 'magical' qualities and practices of Morgan or the other priestesses successfully. However, on a purely human level, their problems with women had a monumental effect upon their lives.

Morgan is a character who is unsurpassed in what she gives us in intrigue and excitement and yet who, at the same time, perplexes and bewilders us entirely.

To begin with, she spent most of her childhood in a nunnery. This perhaps served two purposes, one of which was to ensure a proper education, while the other concerned what it was proper to do with female children who displayed an extraordinary ability for the 'sacred sight' and/or other mystical qualities. Schools designed to educate such young women are found in Malory's *Morte D'Arthur*: 'Morgan le Fay was not married, but put to school in a nunnery, where she became a great mistress of magic.'

Various legends portray Morgan differently, some positively, others negatively, but always as the person-ification of feminine shamanic power. In her positive aspect, it is Morgan who receives Arthur at the end of the last battle to heal him of his mortal wounds. In the negative, she is his enemy, who seeks to destroy him and others out of jealousy and hatred. She is depicted as a despicable sorceress who never hesitates to use her magic for her own self-serving purposes. Her possession of the ancient and magical power places Morgan as the 'polar opposite' of Merlin, his female magical counterpart connected with Celtic spiritual tradition by birthright and by her own personal choice of a life path that would afford her an arena within which her powers could find expression.

The Power empowers. Many have entered into the realms of the Otherworld where the root of the Power grows in the soil of mystery and human consciousness. While individual motives may indeed vary, the result is the same in that the Power bestows upon its wielders qualities and capabilities which enhance the mind and consciousness, allowing them to reach great heights and, at the same time, plumb the greatest depths of the mysteries of life. The Power is the gift of the gods and comes only to those who prove their worthiness. However, it is precisely at this point that the battle of personal choice begins.

In coming to understand the Power we have to realize that it, like Excalibur and the spiritual path it represents, is truly a double-edged sword. One edge of the sword represents the fruits that come from using the Power constructively. Such purposes result in benefits for the 'whole' of one's self, for the community, country and, ultimately, the entire planet. The other involves self and self alone – personal satisfaction and gain, obsession to achieve for the sake of personal glory, material well-being and the like. We see both of these sides of Morgan and they are indicative of several important feminine qualities that are found in the dual aspects of the goddesses in various cultures. This duality clearly shows that, as individuals, we must make choices as to how and why we will use our own power, the power that comes from the knowledge and experience we gain throughout life. This, in turn, will determine the direction, quality and destiny of our individual lives. With knowledge comes responsibility for that knowledge.

Only when we take both the benevolent and evil aspects of the human Morgan into consideration can we begin to approach and understand her 'archetypal' character. But there is a third aspect involved: a purely spiritual one that must be included in the female archetype which Morgan so clearly represented. This feminine Trinity is indicative of the three distinct cycles of womanhood: the maiden/daughter of pre-menstrual innocence; the mother wielding the power of pure life-giving creative force; the grandmother or crone who is the disseminator of the wisdom she has gained throughout her life. This Trinity has been related for countless centuries to the three cycles of the moon and to the three cycles of a woman's human life. The maiden/daughter, signified by the new moon, brings all beginnings and the introspection necessary to cultivate inner wisdom for making a start in life. The mother grows, as does the moon, until it is full. The full moon brings the cycle to completion, relating to the crone, old age and the experience and wisdom gained through experiences in life.

In the Arthurian saga we see this three-fold cycle represented by Guinevere and Morgan, each representing the positive and negative aspects of the daughter, Igraine, and the Lady of the Lake. It is Guinevere who signifies the innocent and beautiful maiden/daughter, the 'white flower', the pure and undefiled (barren) virgin who becomes the bride of Arthur, and who, in some versions of the legends, is a staunch Christian and defender of the Faith. This is why her 'fall from grace' because of her affair with Lancelot is so devastating to all concerned, both literally and symbolically. Her opposite, representing the negative side of the maiden/daughter, is Morgan. She learns the ways of magic and uses them to seduce and enchant and to prey upon the weak and unaware. The Lady of the Lake, who Morgan later becomes, had come into maturity of her body, mind and soul, and was the possessor of the keys of the wisdoms which she passed on along with the legacy of her life and her experiences.

How these energies manifest in our own individual lives will be determined by our own understanding of their presence and our feelings about them, regardless of our personal gender, as well as by our willingness to accept the real nature of the natural feminine force which we all possess. While we are currently experiencing a tremendous interest among women in finding and eliminating the reasons for every kind of feminine oppression, both within and outside themselves, and in fully establishing women's rights, we still are not seeing men, as a rule, coming to recognize their own feminine aspects and qualities. In our Western society men are deeply troubled because of their difficulties in relating comfortably to their own inherent feminine selves, just as Arthur and Lancelot were. It was not Guinevere, literally, who stirred up Lancelot's passion. It was born from his own inner feminine power which he, in turn, was unable to handle successfully. He had an 'image' of the ideal woman which he projected onto Guinevere, for she met all the requirements of that inner ideal. Both men and women do this to this day, and according to the work of Jung this is the greatest cause of difficulty in male/female relationships. We seek our 'ideal' in the other person and they may or may not match that ideal in reality. With Lancelot, as with most men, his world was a masculine one and he was a man in every conceivable way. Such a role suppresses any feminine qualities or behaviour – with the possible exception of sensitivity, and that is expressed only up to a point. Arthur, meanwhile, experienced his queen's barrenness and adultery, which may be viewed as symbolic of his own lack of creativity and his inability to be 'faithful' to the feminine qualities within himself or, worse, to be in touch with them at all. Symbolic evidence of this may be gleaned from his lack of contact with or influence from his mother during his childhood. Guinevere's adultery reflects his own distrust of his feminine self. Neither man was whole when viewed from this perspective. We must all have an awareness of our *dual* nature to be truly complete as human beings.

In the spiritual sense, the feminine force in Nature is the Great Mother who is perhaps best understood through a study of the ancient Kabalistic teachings which form the basis of arcane Judaism. In her book *The Mystical Qaballah* respected writer and occultist Dion Fortune describes the feminine force in Nature as Binah, 'sometimes also called Marah, the Great Sea . . . [She] is, of course, the Mother of All Living. She is the archetypal womb through which life comes into manifestation. Whatsoever provides a form to serve life as a vehicle is of Her.' As we see, the Great Mother is the giver of *form* and the Great Father is the embodiment of *force*. Ancient secret traditions teach us that form binds and disciplines force so that matter can exist.

Monica Sjöö and Barbara Mor in their book *The Great Cosmic Mother* state:

The first 3,000 years of Homo Sapiens' existence was dominated by a celebration of the female processes: of the mysteries of menstruation, pregnancy, and childbirth; of the analogous abundance of the earth; of the seasonal movement of animals and the cycles of time in the Great Round of the Mother. The Gate of Horn is as close as we can come to reading the 'sacred book' of our early human ancestors. And it confirms what so many people do not want to know: that the first 'God was female'.

With the suppression of the Great Mother by Christianity we lost touch with more than the physio-psychological elements contained in the female archetype. We also lost contact with the regenerating force in the universe, with continuity and with the positive aspects of sex and sexuality. We have lost awareness of the transitional energies in the power that transforms seed into fruit and acorn into oak. The role of the feminine in creation is lost and with it an awareness of the *duality* of the cosmos. The world was created by a male God, period. And, wherever we go on the planet we find that most institutions – governments, the military and other orders – are male-oriented and directed, although this is gradually changing.

Returning to Morgan, we find that she, as a human being, fought her inner battles, and they were the same ones that all of us must fight. They concern the most basic of human feelings: love, sexuality, marriage, and that all-important inner 'cause' or motivation for living. Perhaps in meeting these challenges each of us bounces back and forth between our 'good' and 'evil' tendencies. At times, we respond to the Morgan within that is ego, bent only on personal will and power. At other times, we become our own healer and use our personal power to bring balance into our relationships and environment.

Like Morgan, the very name of Guinevere stirs powerful inner feelings and images, some of which rival the negative qualities of Morgan in her darkest form. However, such was certainly not the case in the beginning. Most versions of Guinevere's appearance in the legends tell us that Arthur made a special journey to a place called Carmeliade to help King Leodegrance, Guinevere's father, who was being overrun by his enemies. Guinevere's beauty was legendary and it was that beauty that first captured Arthur's attention.

Also, it was simply time for the monarch to marry, for all kings must consider the matter of an heir. What could be more perfect? Here Arthur had found a beautiful young woman whom everyone thought was the fairest of the fair, the loveliest in the kingdom. She was from 'good stock' and a wedding would serve to bind further a political alliance that was already a good one. But there was a dark cloud on the horizon. Merlin, with his foresight, saw disaster and warned Arthur of a tragic fate if he took Guinevere as his wife. Apparently, however, his warnings were cloaked in the hints and innuendoes to which soothsayers are prone, and Arthur either did not understand them or simply chose to ignore them – the latter, most likely. The wedding took place at Camelot.

One of the first feminine archetypal indications of Guinevere's character comes from the wedding, for she is often referred to as the 'Flower Bride', denoting her purity as well as her symbolic alignment with the season of spring and the rebirth of growth on the Earth, characterized as blooming flowers. However, most assessments of Arthur's queen agree that she was haughty and aloof, perhaps falling victim to her own opinion of herself, as women of great beauty often do. In Marion Zimmer Bradley's novel *Mists of Avalon* the queen is seen as a Christian zealot who is bent on degrading the 'old ways' and on doing what she can to destroy any allegiance Arthur or the court might pay to Avalon and its priestesses or to Merlin and the spiritual code he represented and practised.

Malory's treatment of Guinevere is the kindest, and certainly the most subtle and richest. He describes her as generous in her gifts and in her treatment of the knights, a sort of tragic heroine and one deserving of our pity and understanding for being married to a man that she really did not, even could not, love, yet one that she respected and admired beyond question. Furthermore, it is clear that the writer feels sorrow for her love for a man she could not marry and which brought tragedy to the court and caused the downfall of the kingdom. His pity for Guinevere led Malory to giving the relationship between Lancelot and Arthur's queen a happier ending than the rest of the writers did by suggesting that they were finally united after each had renounced the material world and its pitfalls for the peace and perfection of the religious life.

Another rather unique perspective of Guinevere may be found in a recent novel that looks at the Matter of Britain strictly through the eyes of the queen herself. In *Child of the Northern Spring*, Persia Wooley portrays Guinevere as a 'high-spirited, passionate woman, schooled by her father in the arts of diplomacy and raised to be queen' rather than a spoiled prima donna. Wooley also sees the queen as being well-aware of Arthur's importance and recognizing that he was 'destined' and that she was meant to play an integral part in the great predestined scheme.

However, it is not Guinevere's personality, be it delightful or treacherous, that has earned her a place in history: it is her romance with Lancelot. How this relationship is viewed is determined, once again, by the particular personal and religious values of the various Arthurian writers. Guinevere is seen in many guises – from inspiration to the world's most chivalrous knight to a repentant woman who falls on her knees to Arthur for forgiveness for her indiscretions, and an 'innocent' who could surely not be blamed for falling in love with the perfect man!

'Betrayal' is the keyword of Guinevere's life. While this does not pertain to, and is not limited to, feminine energy *per se*, betrayal is, in and of itself, a powerful negative force that must be dealt with. History has given us many 'betrayers', or 'Judases', as they are called. This definition constitutes a potent archetype that resides within human consciousness and not only serves as an extremely potent human fault but almost always leads to tragedy. Also, it can be the instigator of immense amounts of guilt that can plague the human soul. When we break vows of commitment, keep events and feelings from others, or represent ourselves as someone and/or something that we are not, we are betraying others and, sooner or later, ourselves. Our actions set up a 'persona' which others see and judge us by. The persona is a mask designed by the individual to hide what is real or to *create* an image of what we want to be and are not. Such a mask can be a dangerous trap, for it locks one into living a lie. Guinevere was in just such a trap, as was Lancelot, and the results were indeed tragic.

Some of the requirements for initiation are that we live according to our deeds and that we honour the value of truth no matter what the cost. How often we back ourselves into a corner with our personae. How tragic it becomes when we fail to realize that the persona demands that we live up to it, creating a psychological and emotional nightmare filled with having to keep up the image we have created. With Guinevere it came to the point of having to retreat from the world, due to her inability to deal with the situation any longer. At its worst it was actually threatening her life. There are many ways in which people 'retreat' from the difficult situations they create for themselves by lies, deceit and betrayal. Some allow the ego to become overly inflated to help hide their misdeeds or to compensate for their inner feelings of guilt, while in an opposite response, some withdraw to the point of depression or suffer severe blows to their self-esteem and self-confidence. Fear, too, always comes from such behaviour and that fear can, and almost always does, create imbalance and disharmony in every corner of our lives.

In viewing Guinevere's esoteric role in the Arthurian legends, I found Gareth Knight's view of her most intriguing. He states: 'Not only is she the first lady of the court but she is the instrument of a certain group destiny, for it is through her the Round Table comes to the court.'[6] The reference to the Round Table is in keeping with the legends that say that the all-important symbol of the Arthurian Fellowship was a wedding gift to Arthur from his bride. But it was the phrase 'instrument of a certain group destiny' that caught my eye. The 'group' was the Fellowship of the Knights and its importance in being representative of a Mystery School. Although there may be various levels of meaning within this statement, I understand it to imply that Guinevere is the feminine channel through which the Tradition comes to man, just as with the Lady of the Lake providing Arthur with Excalibur. Further, Knight relates how the queen, by the nature of her position, forms the feminine 'key-stone' of the social fabric of the Round Table. 'For every knight there is a lady.' The idea of this male-female balance is crucial to human relationships, to civilized society, and to secure and harmonious relationships between humanity and Nature. It was the imbalance of this masculine-feminine polarity that was at the bottom of the failure of the Round Table.

Another esoteric view of Guinevere is that she represents a goddess figure and energy. There is a story that tells of her kidnapping by Melwas, the King of the Summer Country. She is held in Glastonbury and Arthur cannot find her for a year. Finally, after raising many troops to assist him, he succeeds in overrunning Glastonbury. After peace has been made the queen is returned to Arthur. In this, Guinevere represents life and fertility and Arthur's rescue of her bestows upon him the credit for bringing the life force back from the Otherworld or 'darkness'. The legend also has seasonal connotations in relation to spring and summer, which Guinevere represents, and the fall and dark of winter represented by Morgan in her negative guise as evil sorceress. This brings out an interesting and I believe an important point that relates feminine energy to Mother Earth and her seasons, just as to the moon and her cycles.

For ages, ancestral cultures have called the Earth 'mother'. She provides food and shelter for all her children; she protects and sustains. As discussed earlier, various groups throughout the centuries have sought to honour Mother Earth through their ceremonies, which were often performed to mark the seasons at the times of the solstices and equinoxes. Nowadays, many people seek to 'reconnect' themselves with Mother Earth through the continuance of ancient ceremonies and by educating themselves about Nature and her forces and trying to live in greater balance with them. An effort to get into better balance with the seasons, for example, is for one to try to align oneself with the pulse of the Earth, the rhythm of Nature. Spring is the time for new beginnings, for the instigation of new projects, new relationships and new directions for one's life. It is the time for planting the 'seeds' of the future in the form of ideas and plans. When summer comes it provides the time needed to perpetuate the seeds that have been sown, to weed out that which is not working, and to till the soil of one's life. Autumn is the time when one will harvest the fruits of one's labour, when long-range projects will come to completion. Then, when winter comes it will be a time of less activity, of rest and recuperation. Most of all, winter is a time for personal reflection, when one can look back over the months gone by to see where there were failures and successes and to spend time gathering the 'seeds' of new ideas, goals and plans for the future. The Winter Solstice is celebrated for the promise inherent within the sun's change of course, to return, once more, to the light.

It is certain that the Round Table failed. Its success required human harmony, honesty and honour and thus it was its *idealism* that doomed it to failure, perhaps from the very beginning. Would it work any better now? I think not. Nonetheless, the Round Table provides us with an ideal, an ideal to which we aspire just as the Arthurian characters did. By looking within ourselves we find the polarity of male and female, always interacting, and, in doing so, always colouring and dictating the condition and quality of our lives. The relationships between Arthur and his queen and between the queen and Lancelot are happening within us throughout our lives. We all have a Morgan within us pushing us to serve our own purposes at the expense of others. We are seduced by material things and by loves that cannot be. Coming to recognize these inner conflicts and learning to realize the difference between devotion and betrayal, love and passion, acceptance and denial, can do much to teach us about commitment and honour and lead to greater understanding of the self and others.

There is little doubt that the women in the Arthurian epic brought tests, dismay, disappointment and grief along with love, intrigue, romance and honour. But the real key to understanding the true feminine force lies within the word 'polarity', that male-female interaction that constantly seeks its balance both within ourselves and in our relationships with others and with Nature. A *recognition* of the presence of the male and female forces within us is a first step towards becoming better able to manifest control over these pairs of opposites and bring them into harmony.

References

1. *Mists of Avalon*: Marion Zimmer Bradley.
2. *The Secret Tradition in Arthurian Legend*: Gareth Knight.
3. *King Arthur and the Grail*: Richard Cavendish.
4. Ibid.
5. Knight, op. cit.
6. Ibid.

AWAKENING ARTHUR!
King That Shall Be

*I've had to fight every inch of my life to escape
royal protocol. I've had to fight to go to
university. I've had to fight to have any sort of
role as Prince of Wales. You're suggesting that I
go back and play polo. I wasn't trained to do
that. I have been brought up to have an active
role. I am determined not to be confined to
cutting ribbons.*

HRH PRINCE CHARLES, PRINCE OF WALES

In November of 1987, while leading a teaching tour of
Glastonbury with some of my students, I received some
intuitive information that motivated me to research the
entire Arthurian legends much more deeply than I had
previously intended to and for much different reasons. But

before telling of that experience and the information that
came from it, I must give some background that led up to
my interest in King Arthur to begin with.

In the summer of 1986 there was international publicity
surrounding an event which had been designed to mark the
conclusion of a major cycle in the Mayan calendar. This
occasion, the brainchild of visionary artist and author José
Arguelles, was to take place at a time purported to be of
great change as well as the time when it was predicted that
the legendary god/prophet of the Mayan ancients,
Quetzalcoatl, would reawaken, together with the principles
he embodied. Arguelles suggested that this cycle would set
the stage for humanity to be able to right the wrong done
to the Earth and correct our dangerous and destructive
romance with the 'myth of progress and technological
superiority'. He believed that an era of 'transformation' was
about to open to us and that it would be a time when we
could, collectively and individually, awaken to our 'true
mind, higher mind, deepest mind'. To commemorate this
important calendric event, Arguelles set up what was to
become an international celebration that he named the
Harmonic Convergence. It was held on 16 August 1986.
Spiritual seekers were asked to gather at a sacred site of their
choice anywhere in the world. According to Arguelles, the
'new' incoming galactic energy would be most intense at
these sites.

The Harmonic Convergence was a huge success.
Thousands responded to the request. Places like
Stonehenge, Sedona, Arizona, the Big Horn Medicine
Wheel, the Great Pyramid and Glastonbury Tor were
chosen by New Age 'pilgrims' from around the world as the
sites where they would celebrate the high energy event of
the century.

For several months prior to the actual date of the

Harmonic Convergence many teachers and leaders from within various groups representative of numerous spiritual paths and movements began to talk about the 'awakening' of several mythological or spirit personalities. All were reportedly 'returning' to the planet at about the same time as Quetzalcoatl, on or around 16 August 1986. Due primarily to my circle of friends and colleagues, the spirit entities I heard about personally were those of Native American origin and included the White Buffalo Calf Woman of the Sioux people, the Blue Star Kachina of the Hopi people of north-eastern Arizona, and the 'spirit' of such respected leaders as Tecumseh, great chief of the Shawnee tribe, Wovoka, father of the Ghost Dance vision, and Degandawidah, famed prophet and leader of the Indians of what is now the north-eastern United States. Of course it was not ever the *physical* resurrection of these figures that was being foretold; rather, it was the return of the *principles* that they and they lives embodied. These principles were returning to the Earth at this time for the purpose of reminding us of the ingredients we must have in order to live in harmony with Nature and with each other before it is too late to turn our errors around, before we destroy ourselves and our planet.

It was during the time in late 1987 while I was in Glastonbury that I received a psychic 'transmission' from a 'source' within myself that I have come to rely upon over many years. The information I received planted a 'seed' in my mind that was to take root in my heart. I learned that one significant spirit 'awakening' had occurred during this special time that had been overlooked, for the most part, by spiritual aspirants. I feel that the time is now appropriate for me to share my thoughts with others, who will be the judge of its merit and implications. The 'awakening' one is King Arthur, the one who lies sleeping somewhere in Great

Britain and who it had been prophesied would one day return, with the principles of the Fellowship of the Knights of the Round Table. I believe that time is now.

Since that moment in Glastonbury I have often thought of the words that Malory claims were inscribed on the black marble tomb before the high altar of the Glastonbury Abbey, the tomb containing the bones found in the grounds of the priory. They read: 'King that was, and King that shall be.' I remembered the title of T.H. White's classic novel: *The Once and* Future *King* [emphasis mine]. The idea of the return of the Arthurian principles of honour, unity, valour and equality went round and round in my head. And after my return home to the United States I continued receiving further insights from my 'source' which have led me to draw some personal conclusions regarding the 'awakening Arthur'.

The reader should keep in mind here that myths do, in fact, shape human actions and motivate human behaviour. Some psychologists tell us that they can and do actually extend our human potential. The myth of King Arthur is widespread and has for centuries inspired, intrigued and set standards for human values. Arthur has become larger than life as a figure who overcame life's obstacles in many ways while experiencing its disappointments, joys and challenges.

Fifth-century Britain was in the throes of a crisis and was sorely in need of a great leader and major change. Our present-day world is also in crisis and no country or society is exempt from the threats to unity, peace, a healthy environment and brotherhood and sisterhood that we all face. We are all challenged by the inequality that exists between the races and nations of the world. The ever-widening gap between the 'haves' and the 'have-nots' hounds the very sanctity of human life. Our sense of values, globally, flies in the face of honour as we continue on what would seem to be an inescapable collision course between our greed for profit and materialism and our ever-diminishing natural resources. As I write these words the television reports on war in the Middle East being waged by a coalition of international forces against Iraq. Our valour seems to have been replaced, more often than not, by a wanton fighting rooted in fanaticism and fear. Almost every country faces internal unrest and discontent with their leaders and their policies.

It is out of such corruption and despair that, in the past, figures have appeared who have been capable of helping to re-establish order and, above all, *values* and *principles* that have turned human consciousness towards a better way. Some of these souls have come from the areas of spirituality and religion, while others have emerged from the fields of politics or science or from within the ranks of common men and women. Some have spoken to the world, others to a nation, a race, or only a community. But they have spoken. And their voices have been heard. They have made a difference. In thinking about the re-awakening of the principles and values of King Arthur, of his quiet strength and his ability to unite a country and the people under the banner of a common cause, I thought about his manifestation of the principles of equality in forming the Round Table. I thought about how the Higher Forces had designated the Holy Grail to descend during his time. I also began to think of the Great Britain of today and of the other major countries of the world. The problems of Britain are surely no more or no less than those of any other nation. The country faces enormous decisions concerning its economic, social and political future. Its future will have to be in the hands of a capable monarch able to work in peaceful conjunction with the modern political forces currently operating. And if not a monarch or political leader, an individual who possesses the wisdom of foresight and enough sensitivity to current world conditions to instigate a change in values and human consciousness. As I looked, I began to see such a figure emerge . . . a modern figure . . . a man of tremendous vision who stands at the threshold of a new century. That man is Prince Charles, the Prince of Wales, the Duke of Cornwall and heir apparent to the British throne.

Hold on now! Let me make my point before you jump to any premature conclusions about what I am really saying. One of the first things I should like to make clear is that I am not saying that Prince Charles is necessarily the reincarnation of King Arthur. While I do subscribe to that particular belief regarding the continuity of life, I am not saying that it applies here or that it has to apply here for my speculations to have validity. Also, I wish to make the point that I am basing my theory, which I will detail in a moment, about Prince Charles and his possible role in the future of the United Kingdom and the modern world on the man, the individual, and on what appears to me to be his code of ethics and personal values, and his sensitivity to social and spiritual issues, as well as his sense of 'vision'. Therefore I shall offer some insights into this remarkable man and leave any decisions about the true nature of his destiny up to the reader.

Charles, the Prince of Wales, was born on 14 November 1948 at Buckingham Palace. Genealogist Gerald Pagent wrote: 'In Prince Charles' veins runs the blood of emperors and kings, Russian boyars, Spanish grandees, noblemen of every European nation, bishops and judges, knights and squires, and tradesmen right down to a butcher, a toymaker, and an innkeeper.'[2] Today Prince Charles is the Duke of Cornwall, Duke of Rothesay, Earl of Carrick, Baron of Renfrew, Lord of the Isles and Great Steward of Scotland,

Prince of Wales, and the heir apparent to the British throne. Yet although he was born into the world's most notable royal family, his mother, Queen Elizabeth II, has always been concerned that her children should grow up as normally as possible.

As he has grown into manhood, Prince Charles has let no grass grow under his feet while he waits to become king. After graduating from Cambridge and spending some six years in the military, he spent 10 years travelling throughout the United Kingdom, learning of the dismal, rapidly decaying social conditions and drawing attention to the pitiful plight of the homeless and the unemployed, and to the stigma connected with those who belong to racial, social, religious and economic minorities. With a clear picture of the living conditions and the low morale of so many people, the Prince began to devise ways in which he could make a difference. Although the heir to the throne may have no political power, he is in a position to influence those who do.

Prince Charles' unofficial biographer, Anthony Holden, describes His Royal Highness in the book *King Charles III*:

I argue that Charles is redefining the office of Prince of Wales. Even more remarkably, perhaps, despite a series of tactical errors, he is also giving the monarchy a contemporary relevance of which it had grown sorely in need. With his interest in architecture and conservation, employment and the inner cities, race relations and other urgent social concerns of the day, he is single-handedly lending the Crown a respectability among the thinking classes which it had lacked for several generations.

It is clear that Prince Charles' interest in the people of his country and of the entire world is deeply ingrained in his psyche – and that just may be somewhat unique given his own comfortable social and financial position. To most of us it would seem like a blessing to be born into royalty. Money being no object, we might imagine travelling anywhere we liked at any time and buying anything our heart desired. Also, there is the attention, the best food, not having to work for a living, lifetime security . . . everything, it would seem, a human being could want. Strange as it may seem, to Prince Charles, it may not be enough. Enough to satisfy any material need for security, of course. But is it enough to satisfy or fulfil a man who really does find himself in that position? In the case of the current Prince of Wales the answer is *no*. For years it was widely believed that the Prince was a lonely figure who was confused and frustrated much of the time, trying to make the best of a difficult birthright. What may seem to an observer an easy life, may not, in fact, be all it seems at a casual glance.

A typical day in Charles' life can consist of long hours of various committee meetings, paperwork and speech writing. In the course of a year there is travel both inside and outside the country and countless public appearances:

> *For a man who cares passionately about the nation over which he will one day reign . . . through his constant travels, [Charles] is in much closer touch with its problems than most ministers . . . The inhibitions placed upon him can prove very frustrating.*[3]

Amid it all, however, Charles has been able to develop a personal philosophy and it is that philosophy that bears examination here, for it is one that is centred around current social, national and global concerns, and it may give the reader some indication as to the basis of my feelings about this man who is in a unique position to someday make his dreams become reality.

One thing that has provided the Prince with a real 'hands-on' opportunity to do something about the social conditions he feels so strongly about is the so-called Prince's Trust. Established in 1976, the Trust was set up to 'help disadvantaged young people to help themselves'. Through the Trust small grants are available to assist in enabling young people to take charge of their own welfare and personal development. Obviously this aid goes beyond purely financial matters and helps provide the lasting value of self-esteem. Also under the auspices of the Prince's Trust, other social projects have come to life. One, The Prince of Wales' Community Venture, is designed to give young people a chance to give of themselves to their local community in a variety of ways, including delivering meals to the elderly and repairing run-down buildings. Charles would like to have this become compulsory. Another is The Youth Business Initiative which is set up to 'educate, advise and support young unemployed people with a view to setting up small businesses of their own'.[4] There is more but the story is the same. For a man who has no chance of changing his job or his lifestyle, Prince Charles has been able to turn his power, at least in part, towards solving some of Great Britain's worst social dilemmas. If he succeeds, then other countries and leaders may be encouraged to follow suit by implementing the same type of initiatives. People are more apt to turn their attention to and take action on issues that are supported by famous and popular individuals, and so Prince Charles has tremendous potential, like King Arthur, to bring reform.

There is yet another side to the interests of Prince Charles that has been coming to the forefront of late. This aspect indicates his awareness of the spiritual aspects of his own nature and of the nature of all that lives. Let me explain. In the words of biographer Anthony Holden, 'An introspective man, with a pessimistic streak, Charles believes that the modern world is on a downhill slope and thinks it only logical to explore alternative solutions.' It is precisely this reference to 'alternative solutions' that has led the tabloids to refer to Charles as the 'loony' Prince.

One of the Prince's views that has brought him negative criticism is his interest in unorthodox medicine and treatment. Even though the royal family has long been involved with the principles and practice of homoeopathy and employs a court homoeopathist, Charles would like to see things go much further, as evidenced in a speech he presented to the British Medical Association in 1987. The speech included such remarks as 'Today's unorthodoxy is probably going to be tomorrow's convention' and 'Wonderful as many of them [drugs] are, it should be still more widely stressed by doctors that the health of human beings is often determined by their behaviour, their food and the nature of their environment.'[5] The results of the Prince's efforts were, at best, bittersweet for though he went on to open a cancer clinic in Bristol which would treat the dreaded disease with herbs, diet and positive thinking, a negative report by the BMA in 1986 had denounced most 'alternative' treatments as harmful.

The environment is another matter that has captured the interest of Prince Charles, as it should for us all. In a speech at Harvard University in 1986 he stated:

We are, to all intents and purposes, embarked upon a perilous journey. The potential destruction of our natural earth, the despoilation of the great rain forests (with all the untold consequences of such a disaster); the exploration of space; greater power than we have ever had or our nature can perhaps handle – all confronts us for what could be a final settlement . . . Over Apollo's great temple was the sign 'Man know thyself.' Could man, at last, begin to learn to know himself?[6]

These and similar remarks have earned the Prince much embarrassment as the perpetrator of 'a lot of mystic mumbo-jumbo'! Now I can admit that the thoughts may have not been worded in the exact manner they could have been. But to say that they are little more than mumbo-jumbo is beyond my understanding.

Such is the Prince's commitment to the environment that in the early 1990s he aired his views in a television documentary, skilfully portraying his wide knowledge of the perils the environment, globally, is faced with, as well as showing his concern for these problems and what they reveal of our human values and priorities. Such statements are a clear example of the Prince's solicitude for the Earth Mother and the future of our planet and all the lives upon it.

It is no secret that Prince Charles has an interest in the work of Swiss psychologist Carl Jung. Jung's views, so it seems, have given the Prince a perspective upon which he bases many of his alternative solutions to human problems. It appears that the South-African-born writer and explorer, Laurens van der Post, has been tutoring Charles in Jung's work, which has given the world a 'system' of thought and principles by which one can interpret and gain a better understanding of human nature. By all accounts, this study seems to have given deeper purpose to Charles' life. Because of it he reportedly keeps a record of his dreams and believes that they have a lot to teach us about ourselves. Also, many feel that van der Post must be credited with helping the Prince to accept his lot in life and to find ways to use it to be benefit of himself and others. This interest in Jung's work and theories, meditation, dream symbology and interpretation, self-awareness, the environment, personal development and perhaps other related studies may not only set Charles aside from his predecessors but is also an indication of an individual who is in search of something that neither money nor position can buy.

Since Charles, as Duke of Cornwall, became interested in organic farming, the duchy's farmland has also taken on a different flavour. This interest has arisen from Charles' deep concern for the environment and is gradually introducing a new and challenging perspective of land use into British consciousness.

However, it is Charles' interest in architecture that has landed him on the centre stage of controversy more than any other of his 'eccentric' ideas. In an account of his views published in 1989 and entitled *A Vision of Britain*, Charles voices his 'deep concern about the effect some modern architecture has had on the environment and on people's lives'. These opinions, first presented by His Royal Highness in his first television documentary in 1988, have won him tremendous public support, although not everyone is in agreement. I have chosen a couple of excerpts from *A Vision of Britain* that I feel give a good insight not only into Charles' motives in criticizing some modern architecture, but also into the character of the man himself.

The first is a defence of his views:

I would like to emphasize above all else that the views I have about architecture, about design and about their relationship to the natural environment of which we are such an integral part, are my own personal views. I do not expect everyone to agree with my opinions. But, if some people feel that they are in sympathy with them, then I am obviously delighted. My chief objective has been to try and create discussion about the design of the built environment; to rekindle an alert awareness of our surroundings; inspire a desire to observe; and most importantly, challenge the fashionable theories of a professional establishment which has made the layman feel he has no legitimate opinions.

On the final page of his enlightening book, the Prince of Wales makes some statements that reveal even more of the inner man. The point is made that even though we are living in the most technologically advanced of times, we gain nothing if we lose our soul in the process and 'forfeit the right to be civilized.'

> Is the earth only for our dominion? Can we or the planet survive the current problems we face due to our own disharmony with Creation? Everything cries out for a reappraisal of our values and attitudes. Don't be intimidated by those who deride such views. They have had their day. Look at the soulless mess in which they have left us all!

Britain's future king believes that architecture is but a physical manifestation of what is within us. If this is true, and I believe it is, evidence indicates that what is inside us may have come to a point where it is dangerously out of balance. Charles and others of like mind challenge us to reappraise our values and principles. We are not immortal in the physical sense and we must not lose the degree of humility which 'enables us to live in gentle harmony with God's creation'.

When we put all of Charles' interests together we see an intriguing image emerge, one much different I suspect, from that which most of us would have expected. But can Prince Charles do any real good? Nowadays the sovereign's functions are primarily ceremonial in nature because the United Kingdom has a government that runs the affairs of state. The ruling monarch merely 'symbolizes' the state and 'personifies' its continuity. Prince Charles is heir to the Crown but it could be some time before he actually becomes king. What can he do? Wait? Hope for abdication, which is extremely unlikely? Presently in his early forties, Charles could be much older before coming to the throne. But does he really need to be king to make a difference in society's attitudes and values? Perhaps it would be better if Charles never became king and continued as he is now – or then again, perhaps being king do much more towards bringing change. Only time will tell. For now, Charles is the Prince of Wales and this position does have its advantages. His voice is being heard.

King Arthur was a man of vision. He united a kingdom. He knew of the natural and the supernatural worlds. He fought alongside his men. When he established the Fellowship of the Knights of the Round Table he saw the value in creating an atmosphere of equality. I am reminded of a remark credited to Prince Charles on the occasion of hearing the standard prayer for the royal family and the Prince of Wales at St Peter's Sunday service, when he expressed the wish that 'they prayed for the other boys too'.

A knight in Arthur's court was sworn to help the weak and the poor alike. He was to stand for and uphold the ethics of the Golden Rule. He was a staunch defender of the Faith. He had to be willing to fight for a cause. Prince Charles has brought some of these most important principles of chivalry into a modern age. Granted, the times in which King Arthur lived are far different from the times of Prince Charles, and some aspects of chivalry have been rightfully abandoned. But should those that remain ever change? I think not.

Also, we must not forget that King Arthur, like Prince Charles, had 'pagan' knowledge, the same knowledge that we now call 'alternative' methods of healing. King Arthur had a knowledge and first-hand experience of the 'soul' of Nature that Charles seeks to rediscover for himself, within himself. To Arthur and the Fellowship, the Grail descended, symbolic of the old traditional wisdoms returning. Perhaps in Charles' time it will, to the benefit of us all, descend again. Perhaps the pursuit of 'unfashionable' and unorthodox ideas and knowledge will become once more worthwhile in the eyes of the masses. While I do not imply that we should toss out the orthodox in favour of the unorthodox, I do support a 'balanced' marriage between the two which can, in turn, be successfully applied to the fields of medicine, psychology, support therapy, the environmental crisis, social problems and preserving ancestral knowledge and values. In the Prince's own words: 'I believe that when a man loses contact with the past he loses his soul.'[7]

When I relate Prince Charles to King Arthur, I do so not so much to compare the two or to unite them in some sort of karmic bond. Rather, I see two 'fated' individuals whose lives happen to have occurred during troubled times. Arthur inherited a kingdom. So will, someday, the Prince of Wales. King Arthur was able to make a difference. So will, perhaps, Prince Charles. But those differences will no doubt be unlike those that Arthur made. Making a positive difference requires, from any of us, *vision*.

When an individual feels or knows that he or she has a 'mission' in life, particularly when that mission involves addressing the difficult social ills we are faced with today, waiting and feeling impotent is surely frustrating, to say the least. Suppose King Arthur had known of his birthright. Would he have been content to wait to assume his rightful role as King of England? I doubt it. There can be little question of Charles' predicament. However, in these times of the 'awakening' of the Old Ones, perhaps the situation will change. If not, the time between now and when Charles becomes king will surely 'season' the Prince. He will learn, as will we, and will continue to grow. With that growth will come increasing psychological and spiritual insights. In the meantime, Great Britain can rest well, knowing that the heir apparent is a caring and concerned man who will, someday, implement measures that will not only make a difference in the state of human affairs but may also be capable of helping himself and others towards seeing the 'soul' in the nation, the architecture, the landscape, the inner cities and, ultimately, each other. Whether he does this because he is the King of England or as a citizen of Planet Earth matters little.

References

1. *King Charles III*: Anthony Holden.
2. *The Lineage and Ancestry of HRH Prince Charles, Prince of Wales*: Gerald Paget.
3. Holden, op. cit.
4. Ibid.
5. Ibid.
6. Ibid.
7. *A Vision of Britain*: HRH The Prince of Wales.

EPILOGUE
The Arthurian Tradition for the Modern Aspirant

Although the legends of the Matter of Britain are fictitious, we can be certain that they are based on human feelings and experiences that are common to ancient and modern humanity alike. No matter how we dissect the Arthurian characters and their adventures we find that at the heart of it all there is one 'force' that forms the centre around which the entire body of legends revolves and which gives it purpose and dynamics. That 'force' is the Holy Grail.

Throughout the course of this writing I have sought to examine the Grail from various perspectives for the purpose of offering a clearer understanding of both the actual and symbolic attributes of this most sacred of all objects. I have come to the conclusion that we, as individual aspirants, have more to learn from the Grail than simply viewing it as representative of the body of the ancient wisdom teachings or of the inner 'quest' we must each embark upon for the purpose of self-knowledge and deeper spiritual understanding. While my intentions are not to diminish these meanings in any way, I think that it is necessary to reduce the Grail's power into one all-important word and that word is *vision*.

I would like to share with you this channelled message from my spirit teacher, Albion, on the subject of vision:

> *Without this specific ingredient . . . vision . . . there can be no spiritual path, no commitment . . .*
>
> *Time and time again, as individual lives unfold, people get a sense which, more often than not, will turn into an absolute 'need' for an experience of a purpose on the Earth . . . We could use the word vision in that way and say that one's purpose is the same as one's vision . . . But let us use [it] in a slightly different way. We will say that vision, to a degree, does involve purpose. Let us also say that vision also involves fulfilment and satisfaction . . . Vision involves an ideal. But, more importantly, vision describes and defines one's way of life . . . When one has vision, one knows what one has to do. Yes, what one has to do . . . there can be no vision without responsibility to it.*

Over the past decade I have been exposed a great deal, primarily through my experiences and knowledge of Native American spirituality, to the concept and practice of the word 'vision'. I have come to understand that, from one perspective, it is a term used to describe a mental image that one receives from spirit forces that may concern and affect one's personal life and future or the future of mankind and the whole planet. Such visions are highly valued by Indian people as they are in similar ancient and modern cultures world-wide. Some Native American tribes honour and practise the Vision Quest as a sacred rite of passage designed to help obtain knowledge and direction as to one's purpose in life. Although the first Vision Quest usually comes at an early stage in life, subsequent quests may be undertaken at any stage along the way so that further general guidance or insight regarding a specific venture or problem might be gained. In such a rite, the supplicant, after the traditional process of cleansing and prayer, goes into the forest, to a sacred mountain, or to some place that is private and holds special meaning, taking only a few necessities. For three days and nights, the vision-seeker fasts, prays, perhaps engages in some personal ceremonials, and laments for a 'vision'. Assuming that the petitioner is successful, the vision may come through a dream, a clairvoyant image, simple intuitive 'knowing' or the appearance of a totem animal who transmits telepathic information to the seeker. Once received, the vision is honoured and is considered to form the backbone of one's personal and spiritual undertakings from that time on.

I have also come to understand and use the term 'vision' to mean a *tool* of imaginative insight about a subject or person or about personal or global conditions. I have known and worked with many Indian medicine people who were considered to be men and women of great vision and, therefore, whose wisdom was much sought after. Sometimes their vision was based upon human experiences, while at other times it was due to their psychic or imaginative insight into the very nature of reality. I am often reminded of the writings of Carlos Castaneda wherein his teacher, the shaman Don Juan, teaches Carlos of the difference between 'looking' and truly 'seeing'. All of us 'look' but how often do we truly 'see' the truth of a given situation or condition, or the nature of another or even of our own self? It requires *true vision* to really *see!*

Upon turning to the dictionary I find that there is yet another meaning for 'vision' that I feel comes closer to describing the use of the word that I have in mind: 'foresight and wisdom in planning'. In this way, vision becomes both the *goal(s)* and the *ideal(s)* to which we, as individuals, aspire. In the Arthurian legends it was the Holy Grail that represented such vision. While the Grail embodied the ultimate goal itself, there were requirements for reaching that goal that ranged from purity in body, mind and heart to the reasons and motivations behind beginning the quest to begin with.

For the past 20 years I have been involved personally and professionally as an intuitive counsellor. During that time I have been asked by what seems like countless persons what their purpose in life is and why they are on the planet. In the early days of my work I was honoured that anyone would consider me capable or wise enough to even begin to answer such an important question. As I grew, however, I came to realize the enormous responsibility involved in answering this sort of question and that, more often than not, the person who would seek such an answer from anyone outside themselves was doing little more than consciously or unconsciously seeking to shift that responsibility onto someone else. Understand that I do think it is permissible, even desirable, once we have come to some conclusion about our purpose, our vision, to seek *confirmation* of it or to desire the opinion of others. But to expect to *receive* a meaningful vision from outside ourselves upon which to build our lives is an indication of lack of self-trust and imagination and, in the end, provides little more than someone to blame our failings on. I have also found that, as a rule, individuals who are dealing with what they consider to be insurmountable problems and who often describe such difficulties as 'the story of my life' are those who have no vision, no ideas and no sense of real direction within themselves. Like the knight, Gawain, these people tend to mimic others or claim another's vision as their own. There is nothing wrong with receiving support from other people in our life quests. But our vision, pure and simple, must be our own.

Once we have accepted the responsibility of searching for our vision we will find our direction. Then, with the vision clearly set in our minds and consciousness, there are many 'paths' that can lead us to realizing it. Such a process or 'path' is clearly contained within the Matter of Britain.

King Arthur had vision. His goals and ideals were monumental. Even though he saw it fail to reach its fullest potential, he knew what his purpose in life was or, at the very least, what it *could* be. He knew he had done his best and had, perhaps without even knowing it, planted the seeds that held the fruit of a Mystery School and that would preserve the Ancient Tradition for modern times.

Arthur also did not let any doubts or fears stop him from attempting to achieve his goals. The first of these goals involved saving his country from invaders and uniting the kingdom under one banner, one sovereign ruler. What good would this desire have done if Arthur had not also possessed the will and personal power to make his vision 'contagious' by rallying around him those who were willing to fight for this cause? And for Arthur, the political, geological and religious conditions of his time made this no easy task, which he would have certainly have known.

Once this goal was accomplished, we see yet another aspect of Arthur's personal vision unfold in his creation of the Fellowship of the Knights of the Round Table. In this Fellowship Arthur gathered around him some of the most enthusiastic, proud and idealistic men the world has ever known. Regardless of the human shortcomings and failures it encountered it was the *vision* of its potential that qualifies this Fellowship as a goal of high standards and ideals. Arthur's vision indicates his keen awareness of the high degree of integrity that humans are capable of reaching and manifesting, and his faith in and love for his fellow man.

Throughout the legends we find the king maintaining that faith even in the face of evidence to the contrary. He fights bravely against the evil in mankind even though, in the end, it pits him against his own son, Mordred. Nowhere is it written that to establish and live up to one's personal vision is easy, especially when it involves the cooperation and understanding of other people. Arthur alone could not make the Round Table into a true and abiding Fellowship. He had to place it into the hands of the group and allow each man his own freedom of action and feelings.

To truly understand Arthur's motivation in forming the Round Table we cannot overlook the esoteric reasons behind his kingship. As stated several times, behind the collective persona of the knights we find the elements of a bona fide Mystery School based on the ancient Atlantean occult wisdoms. Merlin may have brought the seed, but it was King Arthur who undertook the karmic role of carrying it on. We must believe that no organization or group established in the name of spiritual tradition is guarded or protected beyond the merit of its principles. The Fellowship of the Knights of the Round Table must have been, in principle, worthy of existence. I remind the reader of an enlightening quote by Corrine Heline's book *Mysteries of the Holy Grail* shared, in part, earlier on, which I think bears repeating here in its entirety:

> *Wherever there is an occult or mystical group who are honest and sincere, who are working not to amass earthly treasure or to build up a powerful organization but to achieve the greatest good for the greatest number, to bring about the universal understanding that all men are brothers because they are children of the same Father-Mother God, there the Grail descends, and its nearness is known in ever-increasing measure in the benediction of love, peace and beauty, wisdom and strength.*

In the Arthurian legends, the Grail *did* descend and, in doing so, it created the challenge and the opportunity for the knights, and through them ourselves, to learn more about themselves than perhaps the experiences of many lifetimes could have brought. With some of the characters this self-knowledge came through but one incident that spelled success or failure in their Grail Quest! Heline eloquently points out what I believe to be an absolute truth when she states that the 'majority of the knights who came to King Arthur's Court where unable to abide in the high vision of the Round Table'. Thankfully, though, the king's vision was not a total failure, for its ideals *did* give birth to Galahad, who forever stands as proof of the heights that mankind is capable of achieving physically, emotionally, mentally and spiritually. He is the figure of light who is born from the awful tangled web of deceit and lies. In this he becomes the spiritual warrior and hero who serves us well as the role model of the aspirant on the path to higher consciousness.

The aspirant of today is no different from the aspirant of Arthur's time. The same character traits appear to trip us up. The same dragons must be slain. Failures are inevitable but sorrow and pain are the greatest of teachers; they are the 'transformers'. Today we see a rebirth of interest in the ancient wisdoms and the ways of the shaman, shedding light upon the path of highest attainment being travelled by spiritual seekers everywhere. Aside from the chants and incantations, the gift of prophecy, and knowledge of the stars and Nature inherent within the shaman's repertoire, yet another arcane tool is re-emerging into view and is being widely recognized, thankfully, for its value in helping to raise consciousness and in assisting us in becoming more 'connected' to the spirit forces ever ready to aid us in our personal quest to integrate with the subtle worlds around and within us. I am referring to *ceremony*.

Today more and more people are seeking the knowledge of ceremonial practices designed to honour and share in the power of the sun, moon and stars. Rites of cleansing, vision quests, Earth healing and celebration are once more of great interest among the masses. People are no longer, so it would seem, satisfied or nourished by simply warming a church pew. Nature is again becoming the cathedral. Men and women alike are seeking out the masculine and feminine principles upon which the ancient holy orders were founded so that they might become their priests and priestesses in their own right. We have perhaps come to a subtle but real turning point in our spiritual evolution and, if so, it is one where materialistic views and values are slowly being replaced by spiritual ones. Evidence of this may be seen in our increasing concern for the health and sanctity of the environment and our desire to live in harmony with it. It can also be seen in our coming to understand the need for our own spiritual nourishment, and desire to accept responsibility for it, and to know of the nature of the human soul. We are beginning to sense a greater, more conscious awareness, away from those things and actions that lead us farther away from the satisfaction of our spiritual needs. But the wheel of change turns slowly. It cannot be forced. Aspirants must develop courage, devotion, persistence and discrimination, and never lose sight of their personal vision. Through this attitude we come, eventually, to the summit of human consciousness.

During a trip to Glastonbury in 1988, I received a psychic transmission that told of a ceremony that had once been a part of the initiation process into knighthood. In my state of 'openness' I was aware that all of the ceremonial procedures involved with knightly investiture had been held in private with the exception of one rite which was public and served the purpose of celebrating the candidate's acceptance. This ceremony had been called *The Ritual of the Seven Chalices*. It involved the candidate for knighthood approaching an altar that had been set with seven silver chalices that had been filled with water from a sacred well or spring. Each chalice, no doubt reminiscent of the Holy Grail, represented an ideal or quality aspired to by a true knight. By drinking from each sacred cup the neophyte took a vow to aspire to high standards embodied in the moral concepts represented. Drinking also symbolized the internalizing of the wisdom and power of Divine Force to strengthen one's resolve.

In my vision, the first chalice represented the *Gate* of Initiation that one must go through upon entering into a new life lived for the sole purpose of reaching a higher level of consciousness. The second chalice represented the *courage* that is needed to control and overcome fear when facing danger or pain, the courage that gives birth to bravery. The third chalice represented *Nature* as the Earth Mother with all her features and living things. This was to honour and personify the feminine power that produces all life. The fourth chalice represented *unity* and reminded the candidate of the state that comes from being in harmony and agreement with the feelings, ideas and aims of a given group, in this case the Fellowship of Knights. It also stood for the unity in diversity embodied within the Father-Mother God concept which recognizes the interaction of the masculine and feminine forces in Nature and the knight's role in forming the complex whole beyond the Fellowship. The fifth chalice represented *leadership* and embodied the qualities possessed by one whose example may be followed by the masses. The sixth chalice represented *love* in its highest aspect of God's benevolence toward humanity, which may be mirrored in human relationships. The seventh and final chalice represented *hope*, which is born from intense feelings of expectation combined with human desire and which gives rise to the 'cause' of one's devotion. Drinking from the chalices is a 'vow' to the principles that are involved in each one.

I felt a strong need to share this simple but powerful ceremony with others so that it might be used by groups or individuals to celebrate their chosen life's path and to renew their vows to cultivate the seven powers represented. These powers become ideals and goals for better living. I suggest that the time of the full moon is good for holding this ceremony, as well as any of the holy days during the calendar year. If you choose to do it with a group it might be a good idea if one among you is chosen to administer the chalices to each participant one by one. This is also a good ritual to be performed at a sacred site or high energy natural Earth vortex. Although the chalices in my vision were silver, I feel that the kind of cups used should be the choice of each person or group. Once the chalices have been collected they should be cleansed properly, used properly and stored properly for future use.

Each of us is on our individual personal quest for the Holy Grail. Along the way we get the opportunity to observe our feelings and actions. To find the Grail we do not have to adhere to any cult, religion or creed. We must aspire only to the highest good. By serving humanity, we are served. The Grail is everywhere, but nowhere. It is sought by many, but found by precious few. It can heal or destroy. It has no beginning, no middle and no end. The Grail is truly eternal. It binds all together in a bond of love. It is a bridge to the Divine.

BIBLIOGRAPHY

- Artos, Allen, *Arthur: King of Light* (Lorien House, Black Mountain, North Carolina, 1986)
- Ashe, Geoffrey, *The Landscape of King Arthur* (Webb and Bower (Publishers) Ltd., Exeter, Devon, England, 1987)
- - , *Mythology of the British Isles* (Methuen, London, 1990)
- Bradley, Marion Zimmer, *Mists of Avalon* (Ballantine Books, New York, New York, 1982)
- Bryce, Derek, *The Mystical Way and the Arthurian Quest* (Llanerch Enterprises, Dyfed, Wales, 1986)
- Caine, Mary, *The Glastonbury Zodiac: Key to the Mysteries of Britain* (Flexishape, Kingston, Surrey, England, 1978)
- Caldicott, Moyra, *Women in Celtic Mythology* (Arrow Books Ltd., London, England, 1988)
- Cavendish, Richard, *King Arthur and the Grail* (Paladin Books, Granada Publishing Ltd., London, England, 1980)
- Ehrlich, Eugene, Flexner, Stuart Berg, Carruth, Gorton, Hawkins, Joyce M., *Oxford American Dictionary* (Oxford

University Press, New York, New York, 1980)

● Hall, Calvin S. and Nordby, Vernon J., *A Primer of Jungian Psychology* (Mentor Books, New American Library, New York, New York, 1973)

● Heline, Corrine, *Mysteries of the Holy Grail* (New Age Bible and Philosophy Center, Santa Monica, California, 1966)

● Holden, Anthony, *King Charles III* (Weidenfeld and Nicolson, New York, New York, 1988)

● Jung, Emma and Franz, Marie Louise von, *The Grail Legend* (Sigo Press, Boston, Massachusetts, 1980)

● Knight, Gareth, *The Secret Tradition in Arthurian Legend* (The Aquarian Press, Wellingborough, England, 1983)

● Lacy, Norris J., *The Arthurian Encyclopedia* (Peter Bedrick Books, New York, New York, 1987)

● Lawhead, Stephen, *Taliesin* (Lion Publishing, Oxford, England, 1988)

● - , *Merlin* (Lion Publishing, Oxford, England, 1988)

● - , *Arthur* (Lion Publishing, Oxford, England, 1989)

● Malory, Sir Thomas, *Le Morte D'Arthur* (Macmillan Publishing Company, New York, New York, 1982)

● Matthews, John, *The Elements of the Arthurian Tradition* (Element Books Ltd., Shaftesbury, Dorset, England, 1989)

● Mor, Barbara and Sjöö, Monica, *The Great Cosmic Mother* (Harper and Row, New York, New York, 1975)

● Pearson, Carol S., *The Hero Within* (Harper and Row, New York, New York, 1986)

● HRH The Prince of Wales, *A Vision of Britain* (Doubleday, New York, New York, 1989)

● Raymond, E., *The Traditions of Glastonbury* (Artisan Sales, Thousand Oaks, California, 1983)

● Stewart, R.J., *The Prophetic Vision of Merlin* (Arkana, London, England, 1986)

● Tolstoy, Nikolai, *The Quest for Merlin* (Little, Brown and

Company, Boston, Massachusetts, Ontario, Canada, 1985)
- White, T.H., *The Once and Future King* (Flamingo, Fontana Paperbacks, London, England, 1958)
- Wooley, Persia, *Child of the Northern Spring* (Poseidon Press, New York, New York, 1987)

INDEX